1. 3 Horse Ranch Vineyards 🍶🍷🍸
2. Bitner Vineyards 🍸
3. Camas Prairie Winery and Tasting Room 🍶🍸
4. Carmela 🍶🍷🍸
5. Casa d'Acquila
6. Cinder 🍶🍷🍸
7. Clearwater Canyon Cellars 🍶
8. Coeur d'Alene Cellars 🍶🍸
9. Coiled Wines 🍶🍷🍸
10. Cold Springs Winery 🍶🍷🍸
11. Colter's Creek Vineyard and Winery 🍶🍷🍸
12. Davis Creek Cellars 🍸 (Marsing)
13. Fraser Vineyard 🍸 (Boise) 🍷 (Sunny Slope)
14. Frenchman's Gulch 🍶🍷🍸
15. Fujishin Family Cellars 🍸 (Coyotes in Caldwell)
16. Hegy's South Hills Winery 🍶🍷🍸
17. Hells Canyon and Zhoo Zhoo 🍶🍷🍸
18. Holesinsky Winery and James Holesinsky Wines 🍶🍷🍸
19. Indian Creek 🍶🍷🍸
20. Koenig Winery and Distillery 🍶🍷🍸 **D**
21. Miceli 🍶🍷

22. Parma Ridge Vineyards 🍶🍷
23. Pend d'Oreille Winery 🍶🍸
24. Périple 🍶🍷🍸
25. Phantom Hill 🍶🍷🍸
26. Sawtooth Winery, Skyline and Sawtooth Vineyards 🍶🍷*🍸
27. Sheppard Fruit Wines 🍸
28. Snake River Winery 🍸 (Boise) 🍷🍶 and Arena Valley Vineyard (Parma)
29. Snyder Winery, Restaurant and Tasting Room 🍶🍷🍸
30. St. Regulus Wines 🍶🍷🍸
31. Ste. Chapelle 🍶🍷🍸
32. Syringa Winery 🍶🍷🍸
33. Terra Nativa
34. Thousand Springs Winery and Vineyard 🍶🍷🍸
35. TimberRock 🍶
36. Umiker Vineyard 🍷
37. Vale Wine Company 🍶🍷🍸
38. Vickers
39. Vin du Bois 🍶🍷🍸
40. Weston Winery & Vineyards 🍶🍷🍸
41. Williamson Orchards & Vineyards 🍸🍷
42. Woodriver Cellars 🍶🍷🍸

IDAHO WINE COUNTRY

Library of Congress Cataloging-in-Publication Data

Minskoff, Alan.
 Idaho wine country / written by Alan Minskoff ; photographed by Paul
Hosefros.
    p. cm.
 Includes index.
 ISBN 978-0-87004-479-3 (pbk.)
 1. Wine and wine making--Idaho. 2. Wine industry--Idaho. I. Title.

TP557.M546 2010
641.2'209796--dc22

2010010730

Printed in Canada

 **Caxton Press**

www.caxtonpress.com

TO OUR WIVES -

ROYANNE MINSKOFF AND GAYE BENNETT -

AND OUR CHILDREN - NOAH, HANK AND LAURA MINSKOFF

AND BRIAN HOSEFROS.

IDAHO WINE COUNTRY

Written by ALAN MINSKOFF

Photographed by PAUL HOSEFROS

Caxton Press

Snake River American Viticulture Area (AVA)

CONTENTS

FOREWORD

FOR THE PAST YEAR AND A HALF, PAUL HOSEFROS AND I HAVE BEEN VISITING VINEYARDS, WINERIES AND TASTING ROOMS, PHOTOGRAPHING WINEMAKERS, GRAPE GROWERS, VINTNERS AND FIELD WORKERS. WE'VE INTERVIEWED LARGE AND SMALL PRODUCERS IN THE STATE'S EMERGING WINE INDUSTRY AND ENDURED ANY NUMBER OF OFFERS TO HELP US TASTE IDAHO'S BOUNTY. TOGETHER AND SEPARATELY WE HAVE DRIVEN HUNDREDS OF MILES, TAPED DOZENS OF INTERVIEWS AND MADE PICTURES OF SCORES OF PEOPLE INVOLVED IN THE CREATION OF IDAHO WINES.

Early on Paul dubbed my 2005 SAAB "Bottle One." The four-cylinder gray station wagon has taken us throughout the Snake River Plain from Twin Falls to Weiser and transported us to Lewiston, Moscow, Coeur d'Alene and Sandpoint. Paul has photographed vineyards in all seasons, grapes growing in two time zones, pickers at dusk and dawn. He captured images of the sweat and toil as well as elegance and sophistication that define Idaho winemaking.

We've stayed off the Interstate and had a remarkable opportunity to see not just Idaho's vineyards but its farms and orchards, its wheat and hops fields. The Idaho wine road exposes itself deliberately with vineyards clustered along the Snake River, wineries on Main Streets, in industrial areas and out in the country. We left extension cords in Parma and plugs in Juliaetta, traveled dirt roads with only eagles for company and had a grand time. We've learned incrementally by listening to and documenting the people who patiently grow grapes, prune the vines, tend the barrels and wait for the wine to age.

Wine touring is a deliberate act that sharpens the senses. Words that denote taste and color become significant. The landscape reveals its geology and history. Rocks, dirt and altitude matter. Memory revolves around liquid flavors. We have tasted earthy Malbecs in former breweries, classic Cabernets in barns, crisp Rieslings in octagonal tasting rooms, vibrant Viogniers in warehouses, bold Syrahs in lakeside restaurants and ice wines watching a summer breeze. We have tried rosés of every hue and blends that whisper Bordeaux; quaffed ports, dessert and sparkling wines; sampled varietals in virtually every stage of their development from blue-black berries ripening on the vine to the barrel. Paul and I have been treated to some of the most unusual and best vintages that our state offers.

Without exception the vintners, grape growers, pickers, distributors and purveyors of Idaho wines have been generous. They've shared their time, answered our questions and been forthcoming with information. Along the way we've gathered wine lore and legend. Most gratifying of all, we've met and interacted with a group of Idaho originals, who have a passion for wine, and enjoy talking about their handiwork and graciously sharing their stories and vintages with a couple of intrepid wine guys.

For too long the words Idaho and wine were associated with a witty but dismissive New Yorker cartoon and a comic comment from Miss Piggy. With the creation of the Snake River Valley Appellation in April 2007, the consistently strong performance of Idaho wines in competitions combined with the growth of the Northwest—Oregon, Washington and British Columbia—as a wine region, the situation is evolving quickly.

This book celebrates Idaho wine country. Our journey began in January of 2009, when we often heard the skeptical question, "Are there really good wines from Idaho?" After months and months of research, a crash course in palate education, blind tastings and restaurant pairings, we can unequivocally answer, yes. Our hope is that Idaho Wine Country will encourage those who haven't yet tried a wine from the forty-third state to swirl, sip and swallow an Idaho varietal or blend.

We are also committed to the old-fashioned journalistic notion that the pursuit of doing something well, despite toils and snares, matters. In Idaho we have found common ground among the growers and vintners. All are committed to growing outstanding grapes, maintaining solid agricultural practices and crafting the best wines they can. Viticulture is taken seriously and grape growers here benefit from the experience—good, bad and ugly—from Washington, Oregon and California.

Rhone varietals like syrah, viognier and rousanne and Bordeaux blends are making a mark; sangiovese and the look of the Tuscan vineyard have provided a lifestyle model in Boise, Caldwell and Eagle. The traditions of the Old World continue to inform the new. Neither Paul nor I consider ourselves wine experts or critics. Our backgrounds are journalistic: Paul's experience working 36 years with the *New York Times* is both national and international; my career is essentially local as an editor of *Idaho Heritage*, *Boise Magazine*, *Boise Journal* and as a nonfiction writer who's written about the state for four decades. Our endeavor has been to let those involved in the industry tell their stories.

Idaho remains one of the nation's most important and recognized agricultural states. The state's most famous vegetable graces our license plates, is exalted in the media and gives the state an identity as a place that grows great spuds. The state is also known for its trout, has a major dairy industry and remains cattle country.

Fruit growing has a long history throughout the state. The wine country centered in Canyon County's Sunny Slope continues to be a most hospitable place for orchards. Fruit growing has a colorful past in Washington and Payette counties. (At the turn of the 20th century, Payette's semi-pro baseball team was called the Melon-eaters.) The name Lewiston Orchards defined its reason for being, and there was a time when the Palouse was dotted with fruit trees. The return of the vineyards and winemaking to North Idaho brings the Idaho wine story full circle.

Alan Minskoff

LATE AFTERNOON. Hells Canyon Winery.

CABERNET SAUVIGNON VINES awaiting planting at 3 Horse Ranch.

SUNNY SLOPE. Symms Vineyard as seen from Bitner terrace. Lizard Butte in distance.

SPRING. 3 Horse Ranch Winery.

AVA Award-Winning Wines.

CHAPTER ONE

INTRODUCTION

AN EMERGING INDUSTRY

THE IDAHO WINE INDUSTRY, LIKE IDAHO, ISN'T EASY TO CATEGORIZE. THE LARGEST PRODUCERS, STE. CHAPELLE AND SAWTOOTH, ARE OWNED BY LARGE OUT-OF-STATE ENTITIES. MOST OF THE FORTY-ODD ENTERPRISES THAT SELL COMMERCIALLY ARE INDEPENDENTLY OWNED BOUTIQUE WINERIES THAT PRODUCE PREMIUM WINES. GRAPES ARE GROWN FROM TWIN FALLS TO EMMETT AND ARE MAKING A LONG-AWAITED COME BACK IN THE CLEARWATER VALLEY, IN AND AROUND LEWISTON, WHERE THE STATE'S INDUSTRY ORIGINATED 140 YEARS AGO. NORTH IDAHO WINE PRODUCERS, BECAUSE OF THEIR PROXIMITY TO WASHINGTON VINEYARDS, TEND TO SOURCE GRAPES FROM THE COLUMBIA VALLEY. A FEW IDAHO WINEMAKERS USE OREGON, WASHINGTON AND CALIFORNIA GRAPES.

Organic vineyards such as 3 Horse Ranch west of Eagle, Holesinsky near Buhl and Snake River's Arena Valley are beginning to make their presence felt. Just as the movement to drip irrigation has become commonplace in Idaho's vineyards, growing grapes organically is a trend worth watching. So too is the sharing of resources, expertise and technology evidenced in the number of wines coming out of the Koenig's new facility in Sunny Slope and the Urban Wine Cooperative in Garden City as well as the University of Idaho business incubator in Caldwell and the proposed new wine research and distribution center in Eagle.

Both wine tourism and ag tourism are growing. The interest in local foods and the remarkable success of farmers' markets symbolize a regional awakening. The notion that what's raised, crafted and manufactured nearby may be as good or better than what must be hauled or flown in has

taken hold. Add to these promising signs the growth of the wine industry in tough economic times, the recognition of Idaho wines in competitions and the energetic efforts of the Idaho Wine Commission to promote, celebrate and market Idaho wines. Idaho wine country is poised for discovery.

Winemaking and the establishment of a regional identity (an Idaho brand) demand patience. Grapes take time (usually about three years from planting a seedling to producing grapes), and plants need a lot of tending (vine and canopy management are labor and time intensive). Mother Nature is not always a dependable ally (it may be warmer these days but pioneer growers in the 1980s suffered frosts, lost crops but persevered). Our vineyards may be at a higher elevation than those

Above: **SHOSHONE FALLS**. Visitors.
Left: **COWGIRL**. Savor Idaho.

2

3 HORSE RANCH. Bird netting. Morning.

SPRING. Bud break, Weston.

BUD BREAK. Spring.
3 Horse Ranch.

in Napa or Umpqua Valley in Oregon (which is at the same latitude) but have a shorter growing season. Dick Symms, whose family restarted the industry in the 1970s, noted only half in jest that making wine "is a good way to turn a large fortune into a small fortune." Winemaking combines art, craft, science and industry. Some cunning and a bit of luck too.

BACKSTORY

Cultivation of grapes dates back thousands of years (about 8,000 according to experts) and turning grape juice into wine probably was accidental. But the ancient cultures of the Middle East and the Mediterranean had winemakers, vintners and sellers before they had written language to record their skills. Wine has been used in trade, medicine and religious celebrations for millennia. Whether the Shiraz/Syrah grape evolved in Persia or Europe is a matter for historians or archeologists. That the Rhone varietals do well in the Northwest, specifically in the Snake River Valley and the Clearwater, matters to Idaho grape growers and wine enthusiasts. For some Gem State vintners the ancient process—growing grape vines, managing the canopies and the crop, picking the fruit, crushing, crafting the product in vats, fermenting juice into wine, placing those that need aging in barrels and ultimately bottling then selling—is their life's work. For others it is a second career or an avocation.

Above: **SOIL.** Terra Nativa Winery.
Right: **LOVE AND MARRIAGE AND WINE.**
Barrel Room, Woodriver Cellars.

4

. . . the planet's most civilized beverage.

MELANIE KRAUSE. Cinder winemaker checks her syrah before harvest at Williamson.

Winemaking is a time art. All who work in the industry experience the seasons of the vineyard. Life in the wine world intensifies from bud break to harvest into the crush and on through fermentation. Winemakers earn their keep during blending and aging. Here the art of growing wine grapes meets the craft of creating good wine. What Cinder owner and Idaho Wine Commissioner Melanie Krause calls "the thousand decisions" that a winemaker makes exist on a continuum from the moment that fruit reaches just the right flavor, color and level of sugar until it evolves into the planet's most civilized beverage.

For Gem State vintners, it is a passionate pursuit to do something well and create a distinct product that will be bought and enjoyed. Where else do the cycles of agriculture, the processes of manufacturing, the pursuit of the consumer converge with the realities of a culture where the Alcohol and Tobacco Tax and Trade Bureau (TTB) regulates alcohol consumption?

Idaho winemakers and grape growers remain an independent lot who share a passion for excellence. Each wants to make the best wine he or she can. Whether trained at the University of California at Davis' prestigious enology program, at Washington State University

BRIX TESTING BY HAND.
3 Horse Ranch.

Far Left: **KOENIG** and
FUJISHIN Punch.

7

in Food Science or learned on the job, all winery professionals recognize that fermenting grape juice and producing wine takes dedication, know-how and perseverance.

TERRAIN

Viticulturalists and vintners, as well as soil experts and geologists, contend that Idaho's high desert terrain with its volcanic soil, long hot days, cool nights and high-altitude vineyards creates a remarkable environment to grow grape vines. During the cool winters dormant plants store carbohydrates; the temperatures discourage disease and kill insects. Water expert and Snake River Valley resident Jack Peterson says the climate works for grape growing because "the winters are usually not so cold that the vines die but cold enough to kill off the insects." He adds, "The six to eight inches of rain per year allow the growers to control the irrigation." Peterson calls wine grapes Dostoyevskyan. "They need to struggle." Not surprising that one of the newest, and most celebrated wineries in the state chose Cinder as its name.

Southern Idaho's Snake River Plain houses vineyards from Twin Falls to Wilder; varietals are being cultivated in Hagerman and Kuna, Hammett and Emmett, King Hill and Eagle. Recently wine grapes have reemerged north of the Salmon River in Lewiston, Juliaetta and at other vineyards

SPRING. Snake River AVA

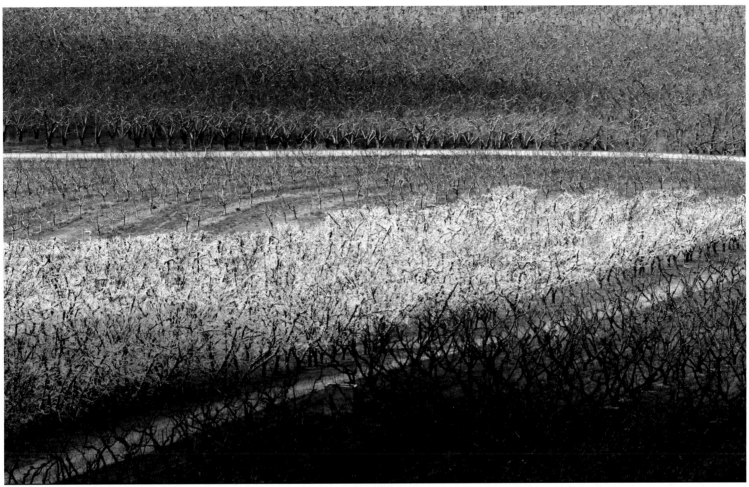

SPRING IN THE SYMMS ORCHARDS off Chicken Dinner Road. Below: **SOIL.**

along the Clearwater. Wine grapes thrive here. Some claim that climate change has helped by lengthening the season so late-ripening grapes can achieve the desired sugars (measured in brix), color and flavor that wines need; others maintain that grapes need heat, light, water, rough soil and tough love. What better place for a fruit that needs to struggle than the alluvial Gem State?

After more than a year interviewing grape growers, winemakers, consumers and wine merchants, it's clear that a renaissance is underway in the industry.

The quality of Idaho wines is being discovered and clearly certain varietals are doing extremely well here. Research continues. The University of Idaho Agriculture Extension at Parma has tested blocks of more than 40 grape cultivars. University of Idaho researcher Krista Shellie, who directs the study of wine grapes at Parma, has published numerous articles evaluating the maturation rates of varietals (from bud break to harvest), looking at water usage and analyzing the effects of deficit irrigation. She has experimental plantings at Parma and at the Sawtooth Vineyard

MICROCLIMATE.

in Nampa. Shellie also co-wrote (with geologists Virginia Gillerman and David Wilkins and grape grower Ron Bitner) an article on the significance of the Western Snake River Plain terroir. This article makes the fundamental case for the singularity of the Snake River Valley American Viticulture Area and documents the geological inheritance that makes the region distinctive.

New vineyards are being planted, the number of wineries has more than doubled in a decade and the success of the wine business in neighboring Washington and Oregon has not been lost on Idaho's grape growers and winemakers. It's not an accident that Moya Shatz, the current executive director of the Idaho Grape Growers and Wine Producers Commission (the Idaho Wine Commission), worked for the Washington Commission, and that many of our grape growers and winemakers meet and convene with their counterparts in the Evergreen state.

LAKE IDAHO

Lake Idaho, the geologic ancestor of the Snake River Valley AVA, rose to a height of 3,800 feet, was more than 200 miles long and 35 miles wide. A catastrophic flood, somewhere between two to four million years ago, was probably caused by melting glaciers that made the lake overflow. Hells Canyon, the nation's deepest, was carved out by this event and its ancient lake bed covered much of what is today's Snake River Plain and provided the underpinning for Idaho wine country.

Snake: The Plain and Its People, Boise State University.

ANCIENT LAKE bed covered much of what is today's Snake River Plain and provided the underpinning for Idaho wine country. Above: Reef built by Lake Idaho in lower Bruneau Canyon.

AVA

April 9, 2007 represents a defining moment for the emergence of the Idaho wine industry. The prospects for Idaho winemakers and grape growers improved in the spring of 2007, when the state earned its first American Viticulture Area (AVA) designation. There are about 200 AVAs in the country administered by the Alcohol and Tobacco Tax and Trade Bureau (TTB). Named for the grape-growing region along the Snake River, the Snake River Valley AVA put the emerging Idaho wine industry on the map. And what a map it is.

With more than five million acres, the Snake River Valley AVA covers an immense swath of 8,263 square miles that stretches west from Twin Falls and includes 12 Idaho counties—Ada, Adams, Boise, Canyon, Elmore, Gem, Gooding, Jerome, Owyhee, Payette, Twin Falls, and Washington, and Malheur and Baker counties in eastern Oregon.

The great Bonneville Flood, which occurred 14,500 years ago and carved out the Snake River Canyon of today, stands as the most important geological event for the AVA. Boulders, silt and sand came cascading through southwestern Idaho and left a legacy of rock-strewn volcanic soil and helped to create the conditions that make the Snake River Valley a very good place for orchards and vineyards.

13

SNAKE RIVER AVA.

What makes southwestern Idaho a good region for wine grapes? It's a combination of geology, climate, topography, water holding capacity, airflow—anything that affects agriculture affects wine grapes. Southwest Idaho's long sun-soaked summer days and brisk nights make Sunny Slope, south of downtown Caldwell, and the Snake River Valley a successful fruit-growing region. In recent years it possesses more than enough heat and sunlight to ripen even late- ripening red grapes such as pinot noir, grenache, zinfandel and the Italian sangiovese and nebbiolo varietals.

14

MEDAL-WINNING WINES

Idaho wines may be arriving a little late at the Northwest vintage party, but they are making themselves known. Southwest Idaho has growing conditions almost identical to eastern Washington, where the Walla Walla region has become synonymous with fine wines, outstanding viticulture and a solid branding effort. Idaho is well positioned to benefit from the international interest in the Northwest wines, wineries and agriculture. Today, Idaho wines and wineries craft more and better wines than at any time in our history. Awards are being won at an unprecedented rate, and attention is starting to be paid. Idaho wines won the highest percentage of medals of any of the northwest states in the 2009 Northwest Wine Summit— Idaho had 63 entries, and the

DAVIS CREEK CELLARS.
Award.

state's wines garnered 47 medals. Five Idaho wineries won gold medals.

Idaho is the Northwest's smallest wine producing region. But the number of wineries is growing— more than doubling in the past decade—as is the amount of acreage now in vineyard. In 2000, there were about 700 acres; now the state has 1,600 in wine grapes. Idaho's industry is producing more varietals, making more cases and selling more wine than ever. In a recent *Seattle Times* article entitled "Wineries in Idaho's Snake River are finally making a mark" wine writer Paul Gregutt argues that before the AVA the state's industry lacked a regional identity, and adds, "But look out world, that region has arrived." A buzz is definitely in the air.

THE NUMBER OF WINERIES is growing—more than doubling in the past decade.

Southern France

THE AVA covers the geologic area of ancient Lake Idaho and lies on the same latitude as France's Rhone Valley.

Southern Idaho

41st Parallel

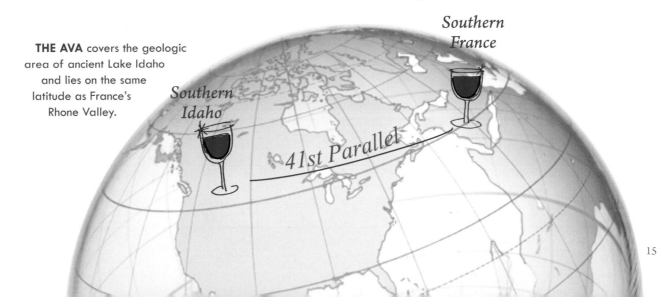

RICH SOIL.

SNAKE RIVER AVA. Morning fog. Lizard Butte in distance.

PRUNING. Bitner Vineyards.

18

TERROIR. Panhandle. Weather, clouds.

Umiker Vineyard. Cool in the shade.

CHAPTER TWO

NORTH IDAHO THEN & NOW

I
IN THE BEGINNING

Idaho wine history begins in Lewiston. While grapes were grown in southwest Idaho as early as 1865, wine production took off in earnest in the Clearwater Valley in the following decade. The Clearwater River Valley in and around Lewiston produced premium wines from 1872 until Prohibition inhibited the industry, first in the Gem State, then nationally.

Lewiston grape grower, wine historian and meteorologist Robert H. Wing says 1872 "marked the beginning of the wine and grape-growing industry that brought fame to the Valley." Pioneer vintners Louis Desol and Robert Schleicher (both Frenchmen) and Jacob Schaefer (from Germany) introduced viticulture and winemaking; the region's wines became widely known. Schleicher, who experimented with 50 varietals, wrote a paper assessing the viability of grape growing in the Clearwater Valley. His wines won gold medals at expositions in Omaha and Buffalo. He won a gold medal at the St. Louis Exposition in 1904, and he believed that the Clearwater Valley had all the makings of a world-class wine region. The *Lewiston Tribune* noted in an Oct. 28, 1908 article "...40 varieties of grapes are grown in Lewiston....Wine made from these took 18th prize among 800 of the world's competitors. These grapes have taken the first prize over California in the last three great world's fairs."

While most wine grapes in Idaho were torn out and replaced with other crops during Prohibition, 1919–1935, there were a few vineyards planted in the 1930s and 1940s. In Lewiston, Greg Eaves made wine from his vineyard in what is now Lewiston Orchards. His "Kueka" wines (named after the famous wine region in New York's Finger Lakes) were marketed under the label The Garden of Eaves, and in 1943 he sold 2,400 gallons of wine. Eaves aged his wines for at least three years, and for a time was the only federally bonded winery in Idaho. From 1942 until he retired in 1961, he was

NORTH IDAHO WINERIES

Map labels: Sandpoint, Pend D'Oreille Winery, TimberRock, Coeur d'Alene, Coeur d'Alene Cellars, Kellogg, 90, Sheppard Fruit Wines, Moscow, Camas Prairie Winery, Colter's Creek Vineyard and Winery, Clearwater Canyon Cellars, Umiker Vineyard, Lewiston

4D

A blast from the past: Circa 1900

LEWISTON TRIBUNE (Jan, 2010)

Vineyard by the river

This old postcard shows a vineyard that was established in the early 1900s near the current site of the Clearwater Paper Paper mill. The vineyard fell out of production in the 1930s after Prohibition outlawed the consumption and possession of alcohol. Readers who would like to share their local historical photos may do so by submitting them to: Blast from the Past, P.O. Box 957, Lewiston, 83501, or by e-mailing them to blasts@lmtribune.com.

THE GARDEN OF EAVES

Idaho Grape Wine

KEUKA

ALCOHOL BY VOLUME 13%

Produced & Bottled by GREGORY EAVES LEWISTON, IDAHO

Above: **FIRST IDAHO VINEYARDS.** Old postcard shown in the *Lewiston Tribune* pictures vineyards that were established in the early 1900s.

Far left: **OSBORNE ESTATE** photo (reprinted from newpaper archives). Left: **GARDEN OF EAVES KEUKA WINE.** Closeup of one of the first wines made, Osborne Estates in Lewiston, after Prohibition.

Lewiston's Superintendent of Parks and his winery business diminished.

Sadly for Idaho's emerging wine industry, Nez Perce County went dry in 1909; the state followed in 1916 and the nation in 1919. Had it not been for Prohibition, the Lewiston and Clarkston area might have become a renowned wine region; that has certainly proved true 95 miles west in Walla Walla, Washington. An agricultural town long known as the home of Whitman College and famed for sweet onions, today Walla Walla has evolved into a viticultural mecca with more than 100 wineries, a revived downtown with tasting rooms galore. Its premium wines have established

LEWISTON, OSBORNE ESTATE.
One of the oldest Idaho state
liquor stamps, ca. 1935.

SABRINA SNODDERLEY, cellar mistress at Beverly's, Coeur d'Alene.

Left: **CLEARWATER CANYON.** Hand crush.

Above: **CLEARWATER CANYON.** Hand crush. Merlot drips into silver bucket.

Below: **CLEARWATER CANYON.** Hand crush. 2009 Merlot.

its reputation and renewed the economy of the city. Walla Walla's well-documented success suggests that viticulture in the Clearwater Valley has a future as well as a past.

CLEARWATER CANYON CELLARS

In 2002, the Asotin County (Washington) Master Gardeners put on a grape symposium; about 30 people from Clarkston, Washington and Lewiston attended. Locals paid attention. Four intrepid couples from Lewiston shared a passion for wines, appreciated their local heritage and founded a winery. The co-owners are Patty and Tim Switzer, Jerome and Jo Ann Hansen, Gary Rencehausen and Barbara Nedro, Carl and Coco Umiker.

Together they are reviving a traditional industry on the Idaho side of the Clearwater Valley. The four Idaho couples met with the group of 30 for a couple of years. The Basalt Winery in Clarkston grew out of this symposium, and the four couples from Lewiston decided that they would start a winery on the Idaho side.

The couples joined together to found Clearwater Canyon Cellars. From the outset they decided that the endeavor would have to be "self-funding." All had day jobs. So, 84 years after the industry stopped in the Clearwater Valley it began anew. In 2004, they moved their operation to its current location on 6th Avenue North in Lewiston's industrial area. They began with all Washington grapes, but recently they've been sourcing grapes from several Idaho growers, much from partners Carl and Coco Umiker's Lewiston Orchards three-acre vineyard. This small winery has progressed from 190 cases in 2004 to 600 cases in 2009.

Partner Jo Ann Cole-Hansen says that growing grapes in the Clearwater Valley makes sense. "We feel that the taste and the grapes from this region are completely different from the grapes from Snake River. A Malbec here and a Malbec there taste completely different...."

She contends that Lewiston, Idaho lets them "make a perfect wine naturally." Cole-Hansen says the low elevation and long hot days combined with a precipitous 30-degree nightly temperature drop allows them "to make a completely balanced, beautifully tasting wine."

"We have the basalt floor that gives the minerality to shape the wine," she says. "It happened a hundred years ago and can happen again."

Clearwater Cellars plans to use Idaho and Clearwater Valley grapes. For now they make five wines. Renaissance Red is made from 75 percent Washington and 25 percent Idaho grapes; this blend of predominantly Merlot mixed with Mourvedre, Grenache, Cabernet Franc and Cabernet Sauvignon celebrates the return of local winemaking. They also produce a Malbec from Washington's Verhey Vineyard; a Syrah; Cab-Merlot and their white blend of all Idaho grapes called Lochsa after the famous North Idaho river. Lochsa, which means "rough water" in Nez Perce, is blended from the Arnett, Ellis, Riverbend and Umiker vineyards made with 50 percent Chardonnay, 33 percent Viognier and 17 percent Riesling. They've also made a Carmenere, a Chilean varietal grown near Washington's Horse Heaven Hills region.

UMIKER VINEYARD

Coco and Carl Umiker grow ten varietals; an "army of two" tends all. Carl Umiker, a University of Idaho soil scientist, says the loam soil resembles Walla Walla's; it has "the same soil that Seven Hills Vineyard is on. Very few rocks, very few restrictive horizons with a lot of water-holding capacity."

COCO AND CARL UMIKER, LEWISTON VINTNERS. An "army of two" tends all.

Coco Umiker, Clearwater Canyon Cellars' winemaker, teaches microbiology at Lewis and Clark State College. She is completing her Ph. D. from Washington State University in Food Science with an emphasis in wine microbiology and chemistry. Not yet 30, she began making wine before she was of drinking age. She and Carl planted their three-acre vineyard in Lewiston Orchards in the spring of 2003. She says, "Lewiston has great potential for growing grapes." She

Left: **COLTER'S CREEK.** Mike Pearson and his wife, Melissa Sanborn, survey the property, which covers 70 acres. They've had to put up a seven-foot fence to discourage deer and coyotes from eating their grapes.

Below: **COLTER'S CREEK.** Mike Pearson lugging a bin.

Opposite: **COLTER'S CREEK.** The vineyard, with an elevation ranging from 800 to 1,000 feet, looks like a North Idaho postcard.

looks for "canopy balance to get the grapes' good sugars and good flavors," and adds, " I like to see balance between foliage and fruit."

The history of this valley matters to Coco Umiker. "We're just redoing what's already been done." Eighty-five percent of Clearwater's newest wines are now sourced in Idaho. A Boise native, she studied microbiology and molecular biology at the University of Idaho. Her philosophy comes down to "style is often dictated by the grapes you are working with…it depends on the year too…sometimes Mother Nature throws you curve balls…You really have to adapt and be open to the vintage year."

She credits a non-commercial winery called Idiot Ridge for getting her and her husband started as well as working at Whitman Cellars in Walla Walla. She also helped out Stu Scott at Camas Prairie Winery while she was an undergraduate in Moscow. "Being a microbiologist I was always throwing yeast into everything." She notes, "It was a lot of on-the-job learning for all of us…for four couples it's pretty remarkable that we're still together."

COLTER'S CREEK VINEYARD AND WINERY

The Potlatch River flows beneath this lovely sloping vineyard. Originally called Colter's Creek by Lewis and Clark, the river was renamed. Colter's Creek owners Mike Pearson and his wife Melissa Sanborn have revived the original name for their North Idaho winery and vineyard located near the tiny town of Juliaetta about 30 miles from Lewiston.

Vineyards were planted on this gently sloping site's southwest facing hills in the 1980s and 1990s. Pearson and Sanborn bought the vineyard in February of 2007 and set about restoring seven acres of historic vines. Most of the vines were cuttings off of Robert Wing's Lewiston vineyard. Sanborn says, "When we bought it in 2007, we cut everything to the ground"; subsequently they've added about three acres of new plantings. In 2009 they had their first harvest and crush.

The couple divides their time between Juliaetta and Moscow. Sanborn went to graduate school at WSU, where she received a Master's in Food Science, specializing in enology; Pearson runs Anatek Labs, an environmental testing facility that tests drinking water in both Moscow and Spokane. They work together, although he does a little more in the vineyards and she spends a little more time in winemaking. She says, "We pretty much do everything together." They have just gone into full production of white

COLTER'S CREEK. Mike Pearson, in the bin, sterilizing buckets before use.

COLTER'S CREEK. Melissa Sandborn and Mike Pearson.

and red wines, have their winery on site and plan to make 2,000 to 3,000 cases and are pricing their wines from ten to twenty dollars.

The vineyard, with an elevation ranging from 800 to 1,000 feet, looks like a North Idaho postcard, has excellent air drainage and is, by all appearances, producing fine fruit. They have ten acres in wine grapes now; ultimately they have the potential for 20 acres. They use solar pumps, have two holding ponds and gravity feed water to their vines. Their focus is on sustainable practices, and they are learning as they go. The historic vines are deep rooted and have produced very vigorous vines causing the vintners to experiment with different trellising systems. For most of their grapes they direct the shoots upward. They are using the Scott Henry system, a method where half the shoots are trained down and the other half up. This type of trellising helps slow the vigorous vines, retards the ripening and pro-

motes higher sugars and lower acids in the grapes.

Their entire property covers 70 acres, and they've had to put up a seven-foot fence to discourage deer and coyotes from eating their grapes. They plan to have about a third of their acreage in whites. The chardonnay and riesling "we will crop heavy about five tons per acre." Among the reds, they hope to do a single varietal cabernet sauvignon; they have zinfandel planted and are growing merlot and tempranillo.

Originally, they were looking to buy property to grow grapes in the Lenore area. On a whim they headed up towards Kendrick and found the site, which Pearson remembers "was a mess,' but grapes had been grown there. The vineyard and winery are located on Highway 3, and the couple hopes that this will be a destination winery. Sanborn notes: "It's a known grape-growing area and has the potential to be fairly big; it's a great area for it. If it's not better than Walla Walla, it's at least as good in terms of degree days." Pearson adds, "We're not trying to make our fortune, we're just trying to make good wine."

Colter's Creek winery sits in a renovated pole barn that they've improved and made into a winemaking facility. The winding road up to the vineyard and winery provides a challenge for visitors. They've contemplated a footbridge across the river to bring customers to their tasting room.

VINTAGE VINTAGE.
Stuart Scott in old photo.

LICENSE PLATE. "Winemaker" is Stuart Scott's. Camas Prarie.

They've been buying grapes from local vineyards in the area and some from Clarkston. They began by blending the local and Washington grapes, but the goal for Colter's Creek is to use all Idaho grapes. Their varietals include chardonnay, riesling, cabernet sauvignon, cabernet franc, merlot, zinfandel, grenache, tempranillo, gewürztraminer, a little viognier and a demonstration row of sangiovese and nebbiolo in their highest and hottest vineyard. They even planted a small amount of rkatsiteli, a white grape that's grown in Russia and neighboring Georgia, which they use for blending. In addition to some unique varietals they use a bladder press for more "gentle pressing"; it reduces the amount of seed tannins. Like their name, their labels honor Lewis and Clark's influence on this part of the state.

CAMAS PRAIRIE WINERY AND TASTING ROOM

Camas Prairie Winery and Tasting Room sits in an 1891 building on Main Street in Moscow, where winemaker Stu Scott and his wife Susan live, make wines and dispense information and knowledge. They moved to this college town in 1981 and settled downtown in 1989.

Stu Scott worked for the federal government as a

parole officer and personal security officer, helping protect presidents including Ford and Reagan as well as cabinet members such as Donald Rumsfeld and Dick Cheney. Now retired from government work, Stu epitomizes the independent-spirited local winemaker who has had to rely on his wits, ingenuity and passion. His historic building mixes green elements such as solar power from photovoltaic cells—that convert DC to AC current—with a variety of handcrafted winemaking apparatus; he's cobbled together all kinds of equipment to make still and sparkling wines.

He has several principles that have informed his operation since he began making wines in 1983. His motto is to be efficient and have integration in the winery. The Scotts believe in "balance in time, space and money." And he has a sense of humor about what he does. "What's a poor man's forklift? A pallet jack. I have two," he quips." My equipment is like me, it's old and ugly." Much of it he's bought smartly and adapted.

Stu says, "Over the years everything has to be cleaned and maintained every time it's used...Air is the enemy of wine so we bottle in a vacuum...we bottle with as little

oxygen as we can, so the wine will have a long shelf life."

What started out as a hobby, while still with the government, evolved into a business. The first paragraph on their website explains:

Camas Prairie Winery is a hobby run amok! First, we grew grapes to make wine to please ourselves. Then, in 1983 a great, small, micro-boutique business! We field-crush at the vineyard, then back to the winery to press, ferment, age & bottle. A true Mom & Pop operation. We even live above the winery.

Stu feels lucky that he's converted an avocation into a commercial enterprise. While he still worked for the federal government until he was fifty, "all the winery had to do was support itself." Starting out in their garage, they outgrew their space and decided to expand. They spent two years looking for just the right spot to live, craft wine and have a tasting room.

Camas Prairie's storefront tasting room sits only blocks from the University of Idaho campus. Moscow is a "sweet wine market," says Stu. They make lightly sweet and dry wines as well, but recognized their market. The only winery in this college town, Camas Prairie has its challenges being in Moscow, an off-the-beaten-path wine destination.

Stu has had to be both experimental and entrepreneurial. The only producer of fruit wines, mead (a beverage made by fermenting honey) and hand-riddled sparkling wines in the state, the

CAMAS PRAIRIE. Solar panels. Stuart Scott in foreground.

winery features
23 wines—five
sparkling and eigh-
teen still. Among
their more unusual
products they
list huckleberry,
wild plum, orange
Muscadet; several varieties of mead as well as traditional
varietals such as Cabernet Sauvignon, Merlot, Lemberger,
Chardonnay, Pinot Gris. They source their grapes from
Washington's finest growers such as Champoux Vineyards
in Horse Heaven Hills. Uniquely, Camas Prairie does not put
the vintage on their wine labels. Stu doesn't want vintages
competing with each other, and he does this to save money
for the wine buyer.

The Scotts (Sue has been doing the books since day one)
simply work by supply and demand. Sue points out "we got
into fruit wines because people brought us wild plums and
elderberries." They experimented with huckleberries because they were brought a large supply of Idaho's state fruit.

Camas Prairie produces about 2,400 cases of wine per
year and sells about 60 percent out of the Tasting Room, 30
percent to distributors and 10 percent to house accounts.
Stu prides himself on making "uniformly good wines" that
sell at reasonable prices. Much of their business comes from
tourists and families coming to visit either the University of
Idaho or WSU in nearby Pullman, Washington.

Named Idaho Winery of the Year by *Winepress Northwest* in 2007, Camas Prairie wines have garnered their share
of awards. Stu is especially proud of the medals from the
Los Angeles County International Wine Competition. The
Tasting Room and the second story loft create an inviting
space to sample wines or select a brew from "the largest selection of imported beers (68 varieties) in Northern Idaho."
Among the unique libations available from Camas Prairie is
a hand-riddled and disgorged Raspberry Brut–made in the

Méthode Champenoise, which he learned during his time in California from winemaker Tom Kruse. To Stu, winemaking combines art and science, with "knowing how to achieve different results."

From the Hog Heaven Red & Hot Spiced Wine to Ewe Eye White (Gewürztraminer), and Sarah's Blush (Lemberger), Camas Prairie's owners have created a unique business model. Stu teaches a Wine Tasting 101 once a month, does custom labeling and makes vinegar. The winery has received its share of acclaim for sustainable practices including a 2009 visit from Idaho Senator Mike Crapo championing the Scotts for taking advantage of a federal grant that enabled them to put in the solar panels to cut energy costs and help reduce the winery's carbon footprint. The solar panels provide about 75 percent of the energy for the winery.

COEUR D'ALENE CELLARS

The north Idaho Panhandle with its soul-enriching lake country, emerald green mountains and maritime climate may lack the degree-days to grow wine grapes, but they have first-rate wineries that add to the story of Idaho wine country.

Coeur d'Alene Cellars sits in an industrial area of the city in a handsome winery and tasting room where it produces about 4,200 cases per year. The winery had an auspicious beginning in 2002. The first two vintages attained ratings of 90 from the *Wine Spectator*. The winery sources all its grapes from Washington's

COEUR D'ALENE CELLARS. A lunch pairing wine and food at Coeur d'Alene Cellars with staff, Kimber Gates (second from right) and her mother (third from right).

33

Columbia Valley and has focused on the southern Rhone varietals—syrah, viognier and recently mourvedre. Why these varietals? Owner and general manager Kimber Gates says, "We find they are extremely well balanced."

The winery makes Cabernets and Chardonnays as well as some proprietary blends. Principal owner Gates cites a year in Burgundy where she learned to cook as her initial motivation for going into the wine business. A Whitman graduate, she worked at Waterbrook Winery in Walla Walla. She earned an M.B.A and is an accountant.

Winemaker Warren Schutz went to work at Coeur d'Alene Cellars in 2004 and became the winemaker in 2005. Both Schutz, who trained at Davis, and Gates are committed to the art as well as the enterprise of winemaking. Gates' mother Sarah Gates, a watercolor artist, has done the labels for the winery using local landscapes and themes. Kimber's parents and sister are also investors.

Kimber Gates' experience has been remarkably reinforcing. She quickly adds that it helps that Coeur d'Alene Cellars wines have consistently "received scores in the low

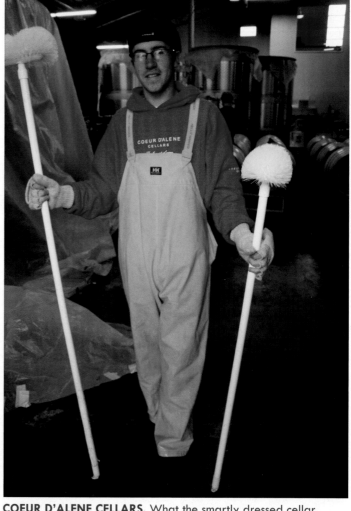

COEUR D'ALENE CELLARS. What the smartly dressed cellar worker wears.

COEUR D'ALENE CELLARS. Wine glass and label.

Far left: **KIMBER GATES**, vintner. Coeur d'Alene Cellars.

BEVERLY'S AT THE COEUR D'ALENE RESORT

From its perch on the seventh floor of the Coeur d'Alene Resort, Beverly's Restaurant overlooks the evergreen rimmed, blue-green expanse of Lake Coeur d'Alene. Named after resort developer Duane Hagadone's mother, the restaurant's wine list runs to 89 pages and its 14,000-bottle cellar is valued at about two million dollars. The floor-to-ceiling wine display presents a remarkable inventory of varietals and blends from around the world. Not long ago a bottle of Chateau Latour sold for $10,000. Eric Cook, the sommelier and mastermind behind Beverly's list, directs their wine program. He works with cellar mistress Sabrina Snodderley who stocks, inventories and organizes the cellar.

Asked her opinion on Idaho wines, Snodderley offered they're stocking more because "they're getting better and we're seeing more of them available." She admires the north Idaho trio of Coeur d'Alene Cellars, TimberRock and Pend d'Oreille but adds, "The wines of [southwestern] Idaho are getting better because there's more of a sense of place. They're making them better." She also mentioned Phantom Hill from Ketchum; recently they've added wines from Fraser and Cinder from the Snake River Valley AVA. She admits, "For a while we wouldn't recommend Idaho wines. That's definitely changing."

CRAB. Beverly's. Panhandle cuisine.

to mid-90's from the *Wine Spectator.*"
And she's found a lot of support from
other producers and from the growers. "We're a real small family here …
and I am really proud of the quality
of the wines."

Their biggest production is Syrah,
which they do in a variety of styles
and blends, from several vineyards;
Viognier and Chardonnay are the
largest volume of the whites. They
focus on several types of Syrah "full
bodied with an intensity of fruit."
They co-ferment five percent Viognier into one of their five Syrahs, which
is a "very typical French method,"
Schutz says. "We do the Viognier in
two styles," one in stainless steel and
the other oak barrel fermented. In
everything, they "emphasize the fruit
and look for balance and mouth feel."
They use some American oak but
mostly French oak in their process.

They sell their wines throughout
the country—even in Chicago—
market to restaurants and fine wine
shops. Remarkably, their wine club
has 450 members; they do 13 wines,
all small productions. Sixty percent
of the wine is sold out of the winery.
Coeur d'Alene Cellars also sponsors
regular tastings and wine and food
pairings at the winery.

BIKE RACK. Barrels at
Coeur d'Alene Cellars.

PEND D'OREILLE WINERY

The Pend d'Oreille Winery and Tasting Room occupies a prominent site on Cedar Street in the heart of downtown Sandpoint, Idaho—about 60 miles south of the Canadian border. The winery takes its name from Lake Pend d'Oreille, one of the Northwest's most scenic bodies of water. Owned by Julie and Steve Meyer, the winery began in 1995. Steve Meyer came to Idaho to ski and stayed to create some of the state's best wines. A telemark skier, he and wife Julie met in California at Cabrillo College, where both belonged to the ski club; he first skied in North Idaho in the early 1980s.

Steve Meyer first became interested in wine 30 years ago when he worked in restaurants in Santa Cruz, California. A chance meeting with French winemaker Francois Milulski took him to Burgundy in 1985 (where he worked the harvest and still got to ski) and cemented a friendship that continues to this day. His stay in France convinced him that he wanted to make wine.

When he returned to the states, Meyer worked at the Roudon-Smith Winery in the Santa Cruz Mountains, where he progressed from vineyard manager to cellar master to assistant winemaker. Meyer took viticulture courses at UC Davis and made his first (amateur) wine in 1987. During this time at Roudon-Smith he went back to school to get a degree in accounting. In 1993, he and Julie, who's from the area, moved to Sandpoint. Briefly, Steve worked for an ac-

counting firm but within two years put together a business plan and began Pend d'Oreille in the industrial park by the airport. After seven years in the industrial area, the winery moved downtown in 2002.

He credits the downtown location as critical to the evolution of his enterprise.

Above: **PEND d'OREILLE.** Sandpoint. Harvest, crush scene. Jim Bopp, top.

Left: **PEND d'OREILLE.** Steve Meyer's hands-on approach to his '09 Cabernet Sauvignon.

"This format has allowed me to take on a completely different role as a winemaker... has allowed us to bring more unique wines to the public," he says, adding, "We were able to be innovative." The Tasting Room sells wine, wine paraphernalia and gadgets but also herbs, spices and "gifts for home, garden and life."

The French connection shows itself in the winery's motto, "Rêves ta vie, vis ta rêves." Dream your life. Live your dreams. A student of local wine history, Steve made a 1999 vintage from the Clearwater Canyon, the first in a century. Steve has a long involvement with southern Idaho grape

Pend d'Oreille Winery has been innovative by responding to the tough economic times. They sell their Bistro Rouge in a 1.5 liter bottle (twice 1.5-liter wines. And it's only for sale in Bonner County." This is a red table wine sold to locals. The winery started this program in response to the lack of glass recycling in North Idaho.

Pend d'Oreille uses the slogan "Think Green - Drink Red." "We think we're the first in the country to do this," says Meyer, "This has turned out to be a tremendous success....

THINK GREEN | **DRINK RED**
PEND d' OREILLE WINERY | SANDPOINT, IDAHO

the size of a standard 750 ml). Steve Meyer says, "Once it's done [emptied], you own the bottle. You clean and bring it back and we refill it; this is intended for people who are buying It's the classic *vin de pays*." The bottles sell for $26; then the wine buyer brings back the same bottle that is refilled it for $16. Meyer adds, "This is truly a community wine."

"Rêves ta vie, vis ta rêves."

growers too. He has bought chardonnay grapes with Kirby Vickers. Both Meyer and Vickers share a passion for Burgundy wines. Steve's also made Malbec from the Wood River Canyon Vineyard in Wilder and made Pinot Noir out of grapes from Indian Creek and from the Kuna Butte Vineyards. To Steve Meyer, the Snake River Valley AVA "represents our own terroir," an appellation that is unique. "The Snake River Valley AVA is entirely about pioneering a new terroir that to a great extent is unexplored; it's like setting foot on the moon."

Steve Meyer believes that Idaho wineries "have a huge responsibility as some of the first consistently available wines to put out top quality, unflawed wine. We're at the fulcrum for where we are going in the future. It's really important to do a really good job now. We create a legacy for future winemakers." While he sees Pend d'Oreille as primarily a regional Columbia Basin winery, he adds because he's an Idaho winemaker, "I like to keep in touch with the Snake River growers."

Pend d'Oreille crushes between 70 and 100 tons of wine grapes a

year that produces about five thousand cases a year; normally they sell about 60 percent of their wines out of the tasting room. Recently in honor of their 14th anniversary, Steve made a Meyer Reserve Cabernet Sauvignon with grapes from the Lawrence Vineyard in the Columbia Valley south of Moses Lake. He began working with the grape grower when the vines were planted. "This wine represents what I am

PEND d'OREILLE. The Tasting Room sells wine, wine paraphernalia and gadgets but also herbs, spices and "gifts for home, garden and life."

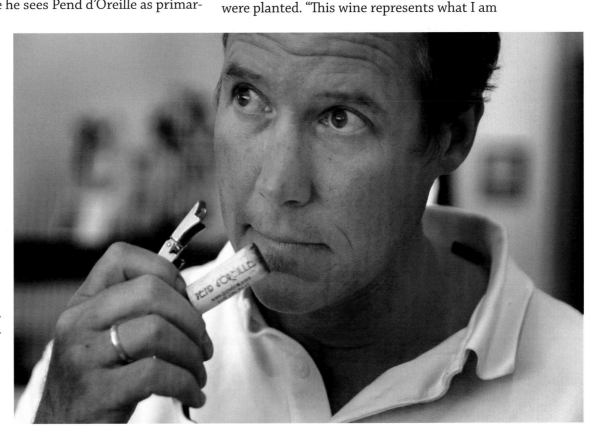

PEND d'OREILLE.
Steve Meyer.

looking for in a reserve tier wine, " says Meyer, "balance between the tannins, acid, fruit." He believes that many a "high alcohol wine will fall on its face."

The mission of the winery has always been to "make world-class wines... to be unique, distinctive and recognizable.... Every time I took wines to Europe the French would complain that the wines were trop puissant—too powerful. I think we have found a balance in the wine industry... won lots of medals... But first and foremost [we] have to be a community member." The addition of the Meyer label and wine represents a "brand that can stand on its own," that embodies a first-rate vintage.

TIMBERROCK

Located on a hilltop in Post Falls, TimberRock Winery has had extraordinary critical success. The 2006 Summit was awarded a 90 pts in 2009 from the *Wine Spectator*. Winemaker Dr. Kevin Rogers (a veterinarian) and his wife Michelle ("Aeromedical Transport health care professional by day, TimberRock party planner by night") have created a first-rate winery in Post Falls. The Rogers are committed to crafting premium wines with grapes from some of Washington's most established and admired vineyards including Phinney Hill in the Horse Heaven Hills AVA.

Their commitment to quality begins in the vineyard. Their website states: "We have established long-term relationships with those winegrowers willing to collaborate with us in achieving our rigorous vineyard

TimberRock. The winery site very near a hilltop in Post Falls, ID.

TimberRock. Labeling.

goals." Little is left to chance. TimberRock selects grapes from small vineyard blocks. The winery uses vineyards with specific soils and conditions to ensure the precise flavors of their wines.

They have also invested in state-of-the-art equipment to insure quality, including a "new, innovatively designed Euroselect de-stemming machine that literally plucks whole berries from the stem. We use a gentle European designed press to extract the juice from the grapes." Their limited production reds come from hand-harvested grapes that are cold soaked, aged in French oak for a year, then bottle-aged for two more years.

Among their current vintages they are producing 2006 Summit, a Bordeaux-style blend of cabernet Sauvignon, merlot, petit verdot, malbec and carmenère. TimberRock's list also features a 2006 Cabernet Sauvignon, TimberRock Trio (Cabernet Sauvignon, Merlot and Syrah), 2007 Malbec, 2008 "Old Vines" Chardonnay, Riesling and a Rosé of Sangiovese.

SHEPPARD FRUIT WINES

A picturesque small town, Harrison sits on the southeast shore of Lake Coeur d'Alene. In the summer of 2009, Sheppard Fruit Wines opened its tasting room in a renovated building on Coeur d'Alene Street.

After ten years making fruit wine in their Harrison Flats home, owners Jim and Julie Sheppard decided to build a winery and offer their sophisticated fruit wines to the public. They adopted the slogan, "No grapes were harmed in the making of this wine" and have quickly educated customers that fruit wines don't have "to be too sweet and lack quality." Jim says, "Most of the time, our customers are pleasantly surprised with its quality and depth. Simply, we create our wines to be enjoyed."

The winery, which the Sheppards built next to their house, is about seven miles out of town. Here in 250-gallon bins, Jim and Julie craft and ferment six different fruit wines. Long-term, they hope to use oak barrels; for now, they mix in some oak chips during fermenting to add structure to their wines.

The Sheppards make about 1,000 cases divided among six different fruit wines. The alcohol content ranges from 12-and-a-half to 14 percent. The first offerings were Marionberry (similar to a Grenache), Raspberry and Strawberry-Rhubarb, which Jim describes as "patio wines" well-suited for warm weather. In the second year of operation, they're also making "a robust Blackberry, a crisp Pear and straight Rhubarb," Jim adds. Initially, fruit came from Oregon and Washington. That's about to change.

Recently, they have contacted local organic growers for their fruit and found some Idaho huckleberries. (Huckleberries are all wild.) Sheppard Fruit Wines now produce vintages that "represent the unique tastes of North Idaho."

PANHANDLE SUNSET at Lake Coeur d'Alene.

PANHANDLE. Lake Coeur d'Alene. Twilight.

COEUR d'ALENE CELLARS. Pumping to top up barrels.

HELLS CANYON WINERY. Grape harvest. Crush.

WILLIAMSON. Pre-pruning machine operator.

Sunset over Ste. Chapelle arch.

CHAPTER THREE

THE HEART of IDAHO WINE COUNTRY— SUNNY SLOPE

T

STE. CHAPELLE

HE STATE'S LARGEST AND OLDEST WINERY, STE. CHAPELLE OWES ITS EXISTENCE TO THE SYMMS FAMILY, WHO BEGAN THE WINERY AND PLANTED ITS SUNNY SLOPE VINE-YARDS IN THE 1970S. SYMMS FRUIT RANCH REMAINS ONE OF THE STATE'S PREMIER FRUIT PRODUCERS; THE SYMMS FARM UP-WARDS OF 4,500 ACRES ALONG THE SNAKE RIVER WITH 3,300 ACRES IN FRUIT AND ABOUT 220 ACRES IN WINE GRAPES.

Dick Symms, the patriarch of the family, remains at the helm of the family enterprise. His son Dar runs the orchard operations. Dick's grandfather founded the company in 1914, and there are still a few hardy early 20th-century fruit trees on the premises. According to Symms, they got into wine grapes in 1971 "to have a crop that could be harvested mechanically." They had their first harvest in 1973 and sold the grapes in California.

Ste. Chapelle was established in 1976. Symms had become friends with California vintner John Trefethen when the two took flying lessons. Trefethen and Symms were walking on the hillside on the ranch and looking down at the lush valley. They drove a stake into the ground and that's where the Ste. Chapelle Winery was built. Boise architect Nat Adams designed the winery building and tasting room, which opened on July 4, 1979 in an octagonal building that's become an Idaho wine country landmark. Bill Broich, who had been making wine in Emmett, became the Symms first winemaker. He had bought grapes from them in 1977; in 1978, they brought his equipment to

SUNNY SLOPE WINERIES

Caldwell
- Ste. Chapelle
- Vickers
- Bitner Vineyards
- Weston Winery
- Hells Canyon and Zhoo Zhoo
- Koenig Winery and Distillery
- Williamson Orchards and Vineyards
- Fujishin Family Cellars
- Vale Wine Company

Eagle
Garden City
Boise
Fraser Winery and Vineyard
Mtn. Home
Glenns Ferry
Sun V
Twin Falls

STE. CHAPELLE. The tasting room and vineyard icon. This is where Dick Symms drove in a stake and said, "Let's build here."

Sunny Slope. By 1981, they were producing 60,000 cases in their small facility. Asked how they were able to make so much wine in such a small space, Dick Symms responds, "Nobody told us we couldn't." In the 1980s, Symms recalls they were doing as many as 125,000 cases and for a time were the second largest wine producer in the Northwest.

Named for the Saint's Chapel in Paris built in the 13th century by King Louis IX, Ste. Chapelle is Idaho's largest winery, producing about 150,000 cases a year (about ten times more than any other producer in Idaho). The winery sits atop "Winery Hill" with a view of the Snake River and thousands of acres

STE. CHAPELLE. Sunday concert.

of orchards and farms in Sunny Slope. It has a large and airy tasting room packed with Idaho foods, wine gadgets and apparel as well as the full complement of Ste. Chapelle offerings.

In 2000, winemaker Chuck Devlin moved from California to Idaho to take over the winemaking operation at Ste. Chapelle and "to make red wines." Trained at the University of California at Davis, Devlin, who owned his own winery in the 1980s (Devlin Cellars in Santa Cruz), had a propitious start at Ste. Chapelle. He began work on a Monday and the harvest started Tuesday.

The winery has gone through a couple of ownership changes since the Symms sold it in 1997. Now owned by

Ascentia Wine Estates headquartered in Healdsburg, California, Ste. Chapelle joins a group of wineries representing a million-case annual production of highly regarded wines from California and the Pacific Northwest: Geyser Peak Winery, Atlas Peak, Buena Vista, Carneros, Gary Farrell Winery, XYZin, Columbia Winery and Covey Run. Devlin notes that with the new ownership Ste. Chapelle now sells in California and about 30 other states.

The Ste. Chapelle winery is worth touring. A popular location for weddings and outings, the winery hosts a summer concert series on its grounds and the Ste. Chapelle tasting room offers one of the largest selections of wine paraphernalia in the region. From oak barrels to large metal vats, Ste. Chapelle has the state's most comprehensive winemaking operation, complete with a lab where acidity, PH and nitrogen are tested.

Under Devlin's direction Ste. Chapelle, whose Rieslings have long been a staple, have gone into "soft reds"—a sweet fruit-forward selection of reds that appeal to wine drinkers who usually only select whites. Soft reds are not simple to make. Devlin points out that the wines "have to be stopped just before they go dry" and adds the wines are "more fruit-forward and accessible." By pricing these wines under ten dollars, Ste. Chapelle has pleased the sales force at Ascentia.

Ste. Chapelle buys all of its grapes: from Sawtooth, the

state's largest vineyard, from the Symms and smaller growers. Devlin and his staff spend a lot of time in the vineyards and pay very close attention to the grapes on the vine. Devlin says "the most important thing a winemaker does is making sure that the grapes arrive ripe. It is the Holy Grail." He adds, "We don't want to bring too many tons out of the vineyard." He believes that the dry Sunny Slope climate with its deficit irrigation gives the wine grower more influence over how much water gets to the leaves. He spends a lot of time on canopy management and cluster thinning.

Ste. Chapelle sells more wine in Idaho than any other brand. While the winery now makes sparkling wines and a variety of reds, a few dry whites and an award-winning Ice Wine, the soft reds and Rieslings account for most of the production. The "soft reds" have had so much success that recently Ste. Chapelle renamed its Chenin Blanc wines "soft whites."

VICKERS

The Vickers vineyards and home are a short drive up Idaho 55 from the sprawling Symms Fruit Ranch and production facilities. The contrast between Vickers and Ste. Chapelle could not be sharper. Nestled on a south-facing, gently sloping Sunny Slope hill, Vickers has no sign, no tasting room and that's how Kirby and Cheryl Vickers want it.

Recently retired from his day job as chairman of J-U-B Engineering in Boise, Kirby Vickers has been making Chardonnay—the Vickers also grow some red grapes—for decades. His wines and vineyards are much admired for his dedication to the art and craft of vineyard management and winemaking. He and Cheryl, who also recently retired after 32 years as a teacher, have developed their vineyard and vintages on their own terms.

The Vickers trained their palates on European wines that they tasted when they lived just outside of Washington, D.C. in the 1970s. After they moved, first to Pocatello in 1975 then to the Boise Valley two

Above: **DICK SYMMS.**
Founder of Ste. Chapelle.

Right: **STE. CHAPELLE.**
Truckloads of grapes at harvest time.

KIRBY VICKERS. Candlelight.

years later, they discovered Northwest wines. By the time they bought their acreage in 1981, the Vickers belonged to the local branch of Les Amis du Vin. Kirby ultimately became a wine judge.

Kirby Vickers, who's an Idaho native, recalls that Idaho wines began to get some good press in the 1980s. "Ste. Chapelle was expanding," so the couple decided to turn their passion into a vineyard and began planting in June of 1981.

Kirby characterizes their early experience as a "nightmare" and credits his neighbors, the Williamsons (whose orchards and vineyards are just down the road), with "saving our bacon because they had equipment."

Vickers Vineyard provides a study in innovation and adaptation. Their vineyard was the first to use two-shoot training with their vines. The Vickers both vividly remember the original planting. They felt fortunate if they could train a row in an evening. The couple learned as they went along. Water rights had to be figured out, posts and trellises added, and wires to hold up the plants had to be strung. They used high-tensile, galvanized wire that Ron Bitner's dad, who worked for the phone company in Oregon, salvaged from old telephone wires. They harvested their first crop in 1983 and sold the grapes to Ste. Chapelle. The crop was 11 tons off of their then three acres. By 1984, they harvested 12 tons off of five acres. Even now, Kirby Vickers does not fertilize and prefers to harvest about three to four tons off his deep-rooted vines.

That original crop paid for development costs and he adds, "Ste. Chapelle was the key to our survival." Survive they did and their traditionally crafted Chardonnays embody a lower alcohol, slightly acidic style that allows for longevity. "This was supposed to be a weekend thing," Kirby Vickers recalls. For the next nine years, the couple commuted to Sunny Slope from their house in Nampa; they built their house above the vineyard in 1990. That year there was an extremely cold winter; they almost lost their personal wine collection and had to cut the vines down to the roots to preserve them. They had no crop but the vines returned in the summer and the grapes returned the following spring.

Kirby Vickers characterizes his 1992 Chardonnay as a "comedy of adversity."

Within a three-day period, he had to harvest, press and barrel his crop. With help from Brad Pintler and Cheyne Weston the crop was harvested, pressed, the juice put in barrels, ultimately fermented and bottled. He even had to borrow a corker.

Top: **KIRBY VICKERS** with container of chardonnay.

Above: **VICKERS.** Chardonnay crush.

Left: **CHERYL VICKERS** helps with the hand pressing. Gauze is used as a liner between grapes and wood barrel.

That year, Vickers' first vintage won a gold medal from the Seattle Enological Society competition, which was "especially gratifying" for Vickers considering the hurdles they had jumped. Kirby Vickers continues to make Idaho wine to satisfy his own taste and standards. He says, "My motivation is to make a valid wine." He defines the style of his Chardonnay: "Fruit is number one. I am going to be a little unbalanced in the fruit, oak, alcohol. And I am going to be a little unbalanced toward the acidic because it [acid] is a preservative."

One of the only winemakers in the region who uses new French oak every year, Vickers adjusts his winemaking to circumstances. In 2007, he abandoned his more traditional approach; he put his Chardonnay through malolactic fermentation but did not filter it. No fan of the current trend to higher alcohol red wines, he prefers 12-to-13 percent alcohol wines. Baer, a second label for their reds, has recently hit the market.

PLUM ROAD in Sunny Slope. Above: Ron Bitner.

Kirby Vickers' experience in distribution is different than most Idaho wineries. He had a distributor who sold their wine in Boise, Sun Valley, London and Paris. Today, he continues to handcraft the Vickers Chardonnay in his own style. A winemaker, a wine judge and a collector, Vickers fashions his wines his own way and on his own schedule.

The Vickers truly do not release their wines before they deem them ready. Kirby says, "We just released our '93."

BITNER VINEYARDS

Ron and Mary Bitner share a vision of Idaho wine country. They live on Plum Road in Sunny Slope, southwest Idaho's celebrated fruit-growing region in the heart of Idaho's vineyard country.

From his hilltop perch, the entomologist/ grape grower/ Idaho wine enthusiast over-looks the sinuous Snake River Valley. When Ron Bitner bought his steep hillside site "for the view" in 1980, wine grapes were not in his sights. He recalls that Bill Broich, the original winemaker at Ste. Chapelle, who built a house just below Bitner's, told him that his south-sloping hillside would be an ideal place to grow "world-class" chardonnay. A College of Idaho grad, who majored in Biology and later earned a Ph. D in Entomology from Utah State

Right: **BITNER.** Terrace View.
Below left: **WINTER.** Bitner.
Below right: **CHRISTMAS BELLS** at the
Bitner Vineyard.

University, Ron Bitner knew almost nothing about wine grapes. He learned quickly. The next year he, Brad Pintler, Kirby Vickers and Bill Stowe planted vineyards and added their names to the short list of southwest Idaho's pioneer grape growers.

Three decades later, Ron Bitner is an accomplished vintner who knows a great deal about wine grapes, has worked on behalf of the wine industry and become a state and national leader in growers' organizations. For eight years, he served on the Idaho Grape Growers and Wine Producers Commission, the last two years as acting director. In that post he led the initiative for the Snake River Valley AVA. The Snake River AVA that Ron Bitner and his allies in the industry achieved is more than just a seal of approval. It's become the take-off point for a growing industry that's

gaining recognition and market share.

Currently he's the chair of the Winegrowers of America and his lobbying efforts have taken him around the country. He's also a member of the Canyon County Economic Task Force that sees Idaho's wine country and ag-tourism as essential to the region's future. The Task Force successfully championed the first agricultural scenic byway in the state. But the Idaho native remains focused on his community. He and fellow College of Idaho alumni Martin Fujishin and Gary Danielson have opened Coyotes, a tasting room in downtown Caldwell.

Since 1995, Bitner wines have been crafted by his Sunny Slope neighbor and winemaker, Greg Koenig. His 16 acres of vineyards both on Plum Road and on Homedale Road produce award-winning wines. Recent medals have come from Florida (a double gold for Late Harvest Riesling), from VinoChallenge in Atlanta (a gold and a silver), and multiple awards from the Northwest Wine Summits and Idaho Wine Festivals. In September of 2009, Bitner Vineyards was named Idaho Winery of the Year by *Wine Press Northwest*. His current plantings include chardonnay, riesling, cabernet sauvignon, merlot, petit verdot and syrah.

Bitner's knowledge of the leaf cutter bee has made him an influential consultant in Australia. Bitner Vineyards recently redesigned their labels. Paying homage to Ron's double identity as grape grower and internationally recognized bee expert, a little leaf cutter bee sits atop the label. Bitner's allegiance to "Down Under" goes beyond pollinators; his long stays have influenced his style of wines. He appreciates the Aussie style and even labels his Syrah, Shiraz.

Wine tourists and gourmands take note. Ron and Mary Bitner continue to build on their vision. Recently, they opened a bed and breakfast with a commanding view of their vineyard near the truffles in a new hazelnut and oak grove.

WESTON WINERY

In 1972, while working for Charles Coury Vineyards in Oregon, Cheyne Weston drove a truckload of grape plants down Sunny Slope Road to the Symms Fruit Ranch. Several years before the Symms established Ste. Chapelle, he had delivered some of the first vinifera to come to Idaho since Prohibition.

Fast forward a few years and Weston (after a stint in filmmaking) arrived in Sunny Slope and approached Ste. Chapelle's winemaker Bill Broich, who hired him immediately. Weston learned winemaking, obtained some prime Canyon County land and shortly planted his own vineyard on Homedale Road in 1981.

His life as a winemaker began in 1982 when he was one of the first wineries bonded by the Bureau of Alcohol, Tobacco and Firearms (now known as the TTB). One of the region's earliest wine producers, for ten years Weston had his wine tasting room on Sunny Slope Road in the building currently occupied by the Orchard House restaurant.

In 1990, Weston and other grape growers suffered a

CHEYNE WESTON. He believes that being closer to the sun creates more radiation and helps ripen the grapes.

hard frost that killed the vines down to the ground. No grapes were harvested. Weston, whose degree from the University of Oregon was in Urban Planning, needed work, so when he heard that Canyon County wanted to have a planning department, "I went in as a temporary thing and ended up staying for eight years." Soon he was hired as a park planner by the City of Boise. He notes he has been "making wine as an avocation for 20 years."

EARLY MORNING MEETING of the Sunny Slope group. Orchard House, north of Marsing.

WESTON. Mélange red table wine. Red wines spend 18 months in barrels.

Today Weston has two vineyards—his original ten acres on Homedale Road adjacent to Ron Bitner's and Bill Fraser's vineyards and a smaller parcel of four acres around his Caldwell home near Lake Lowell. The vineyard off Homedale Road sits at an elevation of 2,750 feet on a site that's among the highest in the northwest. He believes that being closer to the sun creates more radiation and helps ripen the grapes. At his big vineyard he raises chardonnay, riesling and a little malbec. At his home place he grows cabernet franc and sauvignon, pinot gris, merlot and syrah.

Cheyne Weston has French cousins. These old world winemakers have convinced him of the importance of blending. Blending affords the winemaker the flexibility to express the wine's "high and low tones." Weston produces a red blend in the Bordeaux style called Mélange that combines four of the classic five Bordeaux varietals—

HELLS CANYON. Syrah grapes.

HELLS CANYON. Steve Robertson reflected in forklift mirror.

cabernet sauvignon, merlot, cabernet franc and malbec. The red wines spend 18 months in barrels. Weston calls his winemaking "traditional," which means without machines. He quips that in this business, "traditional means poor." Annually, he does between 750 and 1,000 cases of small batches of wine including Cabernet Sauvignon, Chardonnay, Riesling, a Cabernet Franc/Malbec blend, Pinot Gris and a sub-brand called Walking Stick, named after the vineyard by his home. For years he's called his Riesling River Runner to commemorate another of his passions, his 25 years as an Idaho river guide. Weston has a lot of loyal customers; he also sells his wines through the state liquor stores.

Four decades after Weston crested Sunny Slope Road, he continues to make wine and encourage others.

HELLS CANYON AND ZHOO ZHOO

Idaho wines have few champions to match Steve Robertson, who has ceaselessly promoted the state's wines as well as his own Hells Canyon brand. Steve, whose family came to Idaho in the 1880s, trained as a chef at the famed Culinary Institute in Hyde Park, New York; he has been involved with elegant food and fine wine for four decades. He started out in the 1970s as the chef and proprietor of Annabelle's, then Boise's best seafood restaurant. Soon Steve became an upscale fishmonger when he opened an operation on Overland Road called Mussels. Fish lovers in Boise still miss both. But Steve and wife Leslie gambled on a dream.

They bought land in Sunny Slope and planted grapes. Three decades and many accolades and awards later, their Hells Canyon Winery produces what *Wine Press Northwest* editor Andy Perdue calls "wines of great distinction." And their three daughters have entered the business with their own label, Zhoo Zhoo.

HELLS CANYON. Bijou Robertson.

Steve, Leslie and their daughters are committed to producing first-class grapes on their scenic 40-acre vineyard. Hells Canyon winery and vineyard continues to be a work in progress. They began, like most vintners in the 1980s with predominantly white wines, Chardonnays. These days "between 75 and 85 percent" of their output is in reds. Steve says, "I saw the market changing." Ever ahead of the curve he notes "12 of the 37 acres in cultivation are syrah grapes" which he adds do well in the elevation.

What are the criteria for growing great grapes?

"It's obviously the land, the soil, the microclimate, the water availability, protection from bad weather," Steve says. But what's important and sometimes overlooked about wine is "great rivers of the world are surrounded by great vineyards." The Snake River Valley provides "a very rare climate for growing grapes. If this river weren't here we wouldn't be here," Steve says, adding, "We are on the same latitude as Provence, and Roseburg, Oregon... have an incredible four-season climate" and "we don't have overwhelming precipitation." These factors combined allow for the growing of great grapes.

Between 1997 and 2002, Hells Canyon produced its wine in Washington. In his long career, Steve has sold grapes to winemakers in Washington, but these days he produces for Hells Canyon and Zhoo Zhoo and occasionally sells grapes to Koenig.

Hells Canyon has had a long history of success in wine competitions; under their previous label, Covey Run, their

DAWN OPERATIONS. Hells Canyon. Mechanical grape harvest. Flying debris is vines, leaves, etc. shucked from the grapes.

Chardonnay was scored in the top three Chardonnays of the world, as written up in *Decanter*, and had great press in England. Hell's Canyon vintages in 1997, 1999, 2001, 2002 and 2004 won gold medals at the Seattle Enological Society competitions. "We won six golds in six years from three different grapes [merlot, cabernet sauvignon and syrah]," says Steve. He believes that Idaho wines have had to be better, and though he was initially skeptical now firmly believes that smaller yields contribute to better wines. "Since 1997, we've been averaging two tons to the acre and...if we got more than three tons to the acre quality might suffer."

The Hells Canyon wine labels have brought the winery notice as well. "From the first bottling we wanted to do something that represented the area's abundant wildlife," says Steve, so they sought out distinctive western artists. According to Leslie, Steve asked wildlife artist David Hagerbaumer "to recommend someone to do the labels" and "he recommended himself." The results inspired a series of wildlife- and outdoor-themed labels that are distinctive and memorable.

The Robertsons raise chardonnay, cabernet sauvignon, cabernet franc, merlot, and syrah. Steve, who considers himself a farmer and viticulturist, continues to be stimulated and excited by the art and craft of winemaking. Lately, he has been blending Bordeaux-style reds; the Seven Devils Red uses cabernet sauvignon, cabernet franc and merlot grapes.

Daughter Bijou assists him and is the winemaker for the Zhoo Zhoo brand. She and sisters Jaclyn and Hadley, proprietors of the new brand, have chosen a decidedly bold look to their labels. Zhoo Zhoo's description on the Hells Canyon website is worth quoting:

> Zhoo Zhoo is a line of lifestyle wines available in four full-bodied succulent varieties: Claret, Syrah,

SWALLOWS. Hells Canyon tasting room.

Reserve Chardonnay, and Velouté. Zhoo Zhoo labels feature Euro-chic limited-edition artwork by Babette Beatty. We've combined these unique sexy labels with unique sexy wines.

Quite a departure for a winery, whose original brand featured classic outdoor themes and scenes of Idaho history on their labels. Yet the designs may be flashier and modern but the idea to use labels as vehicles for art remains the same. What David Hagerbaumer's classic labels are to Hells Canyon, Babette Beatty's are to Zhoo Zhoo—a powerful and indelible way to brand.

The three Robertson sisters are part of a youth movement in Idaho's wine world that says something about the commitment to making a sophisticated, quality product with a sense of style. Both generations of Robertsons believe fervently in the future of Idaho wines. Steve says, "We've tried to be promoters in terms of brands, labels and world-wide publicity."

The commanding view of the vineyard with the meandering Snake River below and the majestic Owyhee Mountains in the distance makes Hells Canyon Winery a splendid destination. The cozy Swallows Wine Bar creates just the right atmosphere to sample from their long list (about a hundred different wines) of Hells Canyon vintages and growing selection of Zhoo Zhoo wines.

KOENIG WINERY AND DISTILLERY

Greg and Andy Koenig grew up in Ketchum, attended middle school in their dad's hometown in Austria. Greg studied architecture at Notre Dame and Andy went to the University of Idaho. For the past 15 years, they have staked out a unique niche in Idaho wines and spirits. Theirs is the only combination winery and distillery in the state. The Koenigs, who operate their enterprises

WINERY AND DISTILLERY

The Koenigs grew up in the Wood River Valley (their parents own the Knob Hill Inn in Ketchum) and were familiar with Sunny Slope (their mom is from nearby Nampa). They fervently believe in the potential for both brandy and wine. Greg Koenig maintains, "Sunny Slope is a great place to grow fruit. The first-quality fruit is second to none." Andy Koenig believes the fruit of the eau de vie, the brandy sold in clear, slim bottles, benefits from the long sunny days and cool nights on the Snake River Plain. Even though the eau de vie is for sale in 12 states, "it is a small market," Andy says, so they added Idaho Famous Potato Vodka. Recently the Koenig Distillery released Huckleberry Vodka.

KOENIG WINERY.

as separate businesses, share an old world philosophy and are committed "to doing things correctly." Their distillery and winery sits a couple of miles off Highway 55, above the winding Snake River on one of the most exquisite settings in Sunny Slope.

The Koenig brothers built the three-level structure themselves. It is open, airy and remarkably practical. The first-floor double stills gleam copper and stainless steel and look like works of art. Upstairs is a tasting room with a view of the countryside and of the distillery. Two floors below, wine gains age and complexity in oak barrels.

The brothers' affinity for brandy is genetic. Their dad comes from a small town

KOENIG BROTHERS. Andy (left), Greg (right).

in Austria's Tyrolean Alps, where Andy apprenticed for three years and learned the art of making eau de vie. Andy handles the distillery and Greg makes the wine. In the harvest season the two often work together. On their 70-acre property they have 12 acres of orchards in addition to their vineyard. In their four-acre vineyard they grow two different wine grapes—merlot and viognier. And the orchard includes apricots, plums, Bartlett pears and cherries. They source some of their grapes from Bitner but most come from Williamson. Their new winemaking facility, adjoining

Williamson's vineyard, can handle 10,000 to 12,000 cases a year. This is necessary because Greg makes wine for several producers.

Greg keeps busy. He's the winemaker for Koenig, Williamson, 3 Horse Ranch; Gina Davis' wines as well as Martin Fujishin's have also come through the Koenig's facility. In the watershed year of 2009, when Idaho wines began to win an unprecedented number of awards, Greg Koenig's influence was palpable (about 40 percent of Idaho's award-winning wines at the Northwest Wine Summit went through the Koenigs' facility).

Neither Koenig brother has time to rest on his achievements. They are too busy in the orchard and the vineyard, and making their products and in Greg's case doing "custom winemaking." Greg believes that "the wine is largely made in the vineyard. The wines are expressions of the different vineyards." The cash flow from the custom business allows the Koenigs to improve their equipment. "We're one of the only local wineries that has a post destemmer sorting machine... that allows us to do a better job." He believes that "in Idaho yield equals quality; the lower it is the better it is. This is why I like working with Bitner and Williamson." He's also been pleasantly surprised at the

ripeness of the grapes and pleased at the quality of 3 Horse Ranch's vineyards west of Eagle.

The Koenig Cabernet ages for two years in French oak barrels. Their Syrah blend ages for 18 months and they take the term "reserve" seriously, using only the best fruit. According to Greg, they plan "to stay small and focus on quality." They simply do not have time to focus on elaborate marketing campaigns; they "would rather create good products." Koenig sells almost 65 percent out of the tasting room. Greg states, "We make 11 different wines now." All their production is in small blocks. The biggest production is just 350 cases of Syrah down to 75 cases of the reserve wines. They make about 2,500 cases a year.

The Koenigs' reputation is spreading. At the Pacific Northwest 2008 Wine Summit in Oregon, the largest wine competition in the region that includes wines from Washington, Oregon, Idaho and British Columbia, Koenig took best red for its 2005 Cuvée Amelia Reserve Syrah, which was named after Greg's daughter Amelia and made from "the best syrah grapes from the vintage, specially aged in new French oak barrels for 18 months," says Greg.

WILLIAMSON ORCHARDS AND VINEYARDS

When Roger and John Williamson, who run Williamson Orchards and Vineyards, gather their broods for a group photo at their Sunny Slope orchard, vineyard or fruit stand, it takes a wide-angle lens. For this

DETAIL, CRUSH TAPESTRY. Koenig.

WILLIAMSON'S FRUIT STAND

The Williamson Fruit Stand and Tasting Room is a must stop for anyone interested in the evolution of one family farm. The history of the place can be seen on the side of the building where a living museum of agricultural tools hangs. Having a fruit stand that is open daily helps them sell wine, because a lot of

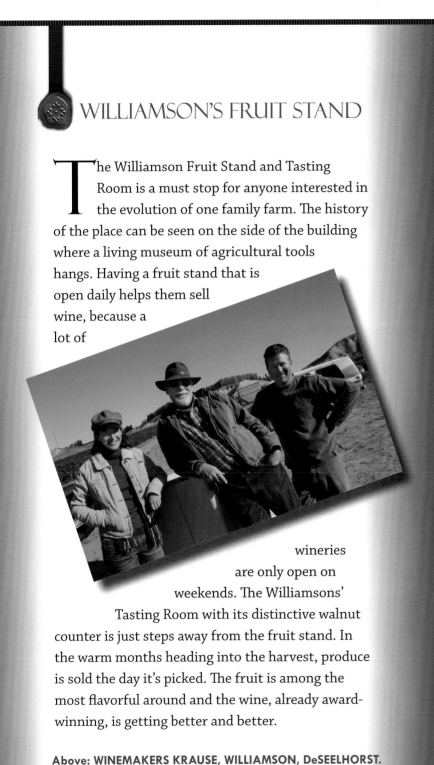

wineries are only open on weekends. The Williamsons' Tasting Room with its distinctive walnut counter is just steps away from the fruit stand. In the warm months heading into the harvest, produce is sold the day it's picked. The fruit is among the most flavorful around and the wine, already award-winning, is getting better and better.

Above: WINEMAKERS KRAUSE, WILLIAMSON, DeSEELHORST.

picture includes four generations of fruit growers, farmers, cider producers and, in the last decade, one of Idaho's premier grape growers. Their award-winning wines begin with their south-facing, gently sloped vineyards. If, as many wine lovers and vintners claim, it all starts in the vineyards, then the Williamson vines and orchards have a legitimate claim to one of the best locations for growing grapes—not to forget apricots, peaches, apples, cherries and plums—anywhere in the 43rd state.

The Williamsons have been growing, packing and selling fruit for decades. Locals swear by their apple cider, which is entirely derived from Criterion apples. Making it keeps this family enterprise busy in the winter months when the fruit stand is closed, trees and vines go dormant, and wines age in bottles and barrels.

The Williamsons' original Sunny Slope homestead was 80 acres. Roger and John's great aunt and uncle planted the first apple trees here a century ago. The orchards, vineyards and row crops now cover 700 acres; about 35 are currently planted in grapes. Roger runs the vineyards. The family got in the wine grape business more than a decade ago when they contracted to grow grapes for Ste. Chapelle. They grow primarily viognier, syrah, riesling and cabernet sauvignon grapes and divide their produce between themselves and other wineries.

Roger Williamson, a West Point grad, and his brother John, who got a degree in agriculture from Idaho, share the responsibility for the multifaceted business. Both their wives work with them, and their children have not only grown up among the fruit trees and vines, they're now integral parts of the enterprise. Susan, Roger's wife, is in charge of the produce, and Ilene, John's spouse, tends the garden. Roger's son Mike works in the orchards and his daughter Beverly works on the marketing side of the business. And John's son Pat is studying viticulture at WSU.

Roger's knowledge of fruit informs his grape growing, and he agrees that the Williamsons' location has distinct advantages. "It has good air drainage, is one of the warmest sites in the region. The soil is a little sticky lower down and sandy higher on the hills—syrah grows well here. The vineyards are easy to take care of. You can grow the fruit the way you want to."

One of their most picturesque vineyards sits beneath the Canyon County Chalk Hills. Roger considered naming his wines after the geological feature but reconsidered because there's already a Chalk Hills winery in Sonoma.

Roger oversees the management of the vineyards and supervises the pruning, leaf stripping, shoot thinning and all the stages from bud break to harvest and beyond. They handpick the grapes for their own wines, as well as Koenig's and Cinder's—about 20 percent of their production; the remaining 80 percent they machine-pick and sell to Ste. Chapelle.

Always innovative, Williamson Orchards and Vineyards introduced Criterion and Honey Crisp apples to Idaho; they also were the first to produce pluots—a cross between apricots and plums—and they're now adding some new varietals to their grape production with blocks of mourvedre and sangiovese.

SMILES IN THE VINEYARD.
Williamson.

WILLIAMSON. Pre-pruning.

Until now, their wines have essentially been single varietals, but blending is in their future. They may only sell around a thousand cases of wine a year but their vineyards are producing varietals for many of the region's best wines. Asked what contributes to a fine wine and Roger says, "It's a combination of great grapes and great winemaking." And he prefers fruit-forward wines that are less tannic.

Williamson produces Viognier, Syrah, Riesling, Cabernet Sauvignon as well as a Late Harvest Viognier (the grapes for the 2007 were picked the day before the first frost) and Doce, a dessert wine that's 80 percent syrah and 20 percent cabernet sauvignon and resembles a port.

FRASER WINERY AND VINEYARD

The capital city's first winery sits in an industrial area not far from Anne Morrison Park. Often linked with the new wave of Idaho winemakers—Melanie Krause of Cinder, Gina Davis of Davis Creek and Mike Crowley of Syringa—Fraser's wines may be recent, but winemaking and grape growing are a second career for Bill Fraser. For decades he ran a successful construction company.

Fraser's former construction office now houses the winery and tasting room. A wine lover and collector, Fraser had long been interested in growing wine grapes and making wine. In 2003, he found a five-acre site in Canyon County on Homedale Road. At 2,700 feet Fraser's vineyard sits at "the highest point in Canyon County where you can see the Blues, the Owyhees and Bogus," he says. Fraser planted three of the acres, then built a casita with a patio. Committed to advanced farming principles, he drip irrigates and uses a vertical shoot positioning (VSP) trellis system.

BILL FRASER. Harvest.

After he retired from construction, Fraser says he went into winemaking because he "didn't play golf and needed something to keep me occupied." He's gotten his wish.

He raises three of the five classic Bordeaux varietals—cabernet sauvignon, merlot and petit verdot—and the winery makes three red wines and an Idaho Viognier. His first release was his 2005 Cabernet, a blend of 90 percent cabernet sauvignon with 5 percent merlot and 5 percent petit verdot. (To be called Cabernet Sauvignon the wine must contain at least 75 percent cabernet sauvignon grapes.)

With help from his wife Bev, two stepdaughters, friends and a hired crew at the harvest, Fraser tends the vineyard, harvests, crushes and destems the grapes in Canyon County, but the wine is barrel-aged—the reds for two years—and bottled in Boise at the winery.

A Boise native and Dartmouth grad, Bill Fraser remains a student. His office is strewn with wine books and publications; he has taken a winemaking course at University of California at Davis. Even so, he wondered whether he would be able to sell his first vintage. Not to worry. His wines have sold well. Last year's Idaho Viognier is all gone as is his initial Cabernet. Recently, Beverly's at the Coeur d'Alene Resort gave him his largest order to date.

Fraser often attends workshops with Washington and Idaho grape growers. He believes Washington winemakers use comparable practices to Idaho (growing their grapes from rootstocks unlike California, where grapes are grafted onto plants) and sees a lot of similarity between vintners in eastern Washington and Idaho. In both regions, long sunny days and cool nights as well as sandy soils combine to give growers excellent conditions.

Most Idaho vineyards also grow their vines two stems up (in case winter kill takes out one of them), use similar varietals and fortunately (perhaps because of harder winters) have not been plagued by Phylloxera (root louse), which has caused so much damage in California. He believes the microclimate of his hilltop vineyard in Sunny Slope is special. The sun rises and comes over the Boise Front and lingers long into the evening. Fraser adds, "People don't realize we have 3000-degree days as much as the Napa Valley and more than Oregon." The Washington growers claim they have two more

FRASER at work in Boise winery; Hailey, his English setter, assists.

hours of sunlight than in Napa; it's similar here.

Grape growing and winemaking may be a second career for Fraser, but his attention to detail and commitment to craft have given him high-profile admirers locally. They include the Grape Escape's Pug Ostling, who says Fraser's "just getting better and better; it took Idaho winemakers a long time 'to dance with the dirt.' They've got it down now; the thing is that wines are like winemakers. Fraser's have finesse, they're big and fit but don't overpower you. They linger. Like Bill, they have quiet strength."

Fraser's distinctive wine bottles sport the Fraser family tartan on their labels. A boutique operation, the Fraser Winery produces about five hundred cases a year that are offered locally and quickly sell out.

According to Ostling, "Wine is raising the civility of life in Boise," and that's worth a twirl, a sniff and a sip—and a visit to Boise's first winery.

FUJISHIN FAMILY CELLARS

Martin Fujishin grew up on a farm near the Snake River. A College of Idaho graduate, he's been in the wine business in various guises (sales, vineyard management, promotion) for more than six years. Currently, he's making wine under his own label (and works with Greg Koenig); he's also teaching courses in viticulture at Treasure Valley Community College and managing the area's newest tasting room, Coyotes in downtown Caldwell.

Fujishin first worked for the Koenigs in their tasting room for almost four years. He and Gina Davis (coincidently the first two winery tenants at the University of Idaho's business incubator on Chicago Street in Caldwell) worked together at Koenigs, which has become a kind of breeding ground for some of Idaho's new wave of young winemakers. After a stint working with troubled youth, Fujishin went to work as vineyard manager for Ron Bitner and soon began to assist at Koenig's winemaking operation. In traditional fashion, Fujishin was paid

in part in grapes and barrels. He has also taken some classes at Davis online.

While he admires and is influenced by Greg Koenig, they do have some stylistic differences. Fujishin prefers to make unoaked Chardonnay. He thinks, "Idaho makes some outstanding Syrahs." He's focusing on Syrah, Viognier and Late Harvest Chardonnay. His initial release was around 700 cases with plans to grow to around 1,000. "For now I am taking most of my grapes from Bitner," he says. He's also making the wines for Bitner's second brand.

Tammy Stowe (of Indian Creek) designed his label, which Fujishin says speaks to both the camaraderie in the industry and the fact that with the exception of Chuck Devlin "everybody in the wine industry did something else before." He believes that wine resembles the winemaker; he points to his mentor Greg Koenig and says if he had one word to describe Koenig's style it's "precise."

With his variety of roles—assistant winemaker, vineyard manager, retail operator—in the wine country, Martin Fujishin understands how important marketing is: "What it's all about is telling your story."

WINE BAR. Coyotes, Caldwell.

FUJISHIN. Sterilizing.

MARTIN FUJISHIN. He is among Idaho's new wave of young winemakers.

VALE WINE COMPANY

John Danielson grows grapes in Vale, Oregon and makes wine in Caldwell at the University of Idaho incubator. His vineyard is in the Snake River Valley AVA just across the border at the Vale View vineyard. Danielson and his partners planted their vineyard in 2007. They harvested their first grapes this past year and their initial wines were a Chardonnay and a dry Riesling; reds are soon to be released. He plans to make his reds in a Washington style, blending Syrah in with the typical Bordeaux varietals.

Danielson's partners asked him to manage the winery and vineyard, where Vale's experimenting with six varietals—merlot, cabernet sauvignon, nebbiolo, riesling, viognier and cabernet franc. He's taken the winemaking certification courses at Davis and interviewed people in the business. Vale's initial release was 250 cases of Dry Riesling and 150 cases of Chardonnay.

These offerings came from purchased grapes. "Our target is to be between 1,500 and 3,000 cases; our goal is not to be big but to be good," Danielson says. A fourth-generation Idahoan, Danielson is very bullish on the Snake River Valley AVA, and he's appreciative of the pioneer winemakers. "You have to take your hat off to the Stowes, Pintlers, Symms, Vickers, and Robertsons. They planted grapes when grapes weren't cool," he says. "I have never found any group of people who are so willing to share with you."

Danielson believes that Idaho wineries are now on a quest for excellence. "There are enough wineries here now and enough people that everyone is searching for quality." He firmly believes that the state of the industry in Idaho "is going up and up. We are just reaching critical mass where everyone is going to take it to the next level." He adds, "Wine years are kind of like dog years because you get one month a year when you are preparing and it takes years to see how I do. I wish I was in this business 20 years ago."

Vale is being noticed. Remarkably, both their first offerings—Dry Riesling and Chardonnay—won gold medals for the 2008 Idaho Wine Competition. The 2008 Dry Riesling won a gold from the 2009 Northwest Wine Summit; the 2008 Chardonnay took silver at the same competition.

Recently, Danielson joined two other College of Idaho grads in founding Coyotes, the downtown Caldwell tasting room that features Bitner, Fujishin and Vale Wine Company vintages.

SUNSET. Snake River AVA. Vale, Oregon in distance at horizon's right.

KOENIG WINERY. Steam cleaning crush.

PLANTING at 3 Horse Ranch.

Rainbow. Sunny Slope.

Bitner Vineyards. Snake River AVA.

Dawn Harvest. Williamson Vineyards.

Dawn. Parma Ridge Vineyard.

CHAPTER FOUR

PARMA, WILDER, AND MARSING

MICELI

LOCATED NEAR GIVENS HOT SPRINGS, MICELI IS THE ONLY WINERY IN OWYHEE COUNTY. OWNER JIM MITCHELL NAMED THE WINERY AFTER HIS GRANDFATHER FRANCESCO MICELI, WHO IMMIGRATED TO THE STATES FROM SICILY THEN CHANGED HIS NAME TO FRANK MITCHELL. HIS GRANDFATHER'S PHOTO, RESPLENDENT IN AN ITALIAN MILITARY UNIFORM, GRACES THE WINE LABEL. FRANK MITCHELL'S FAVORITE TOAST, *"CENT ANNI" (A HUNDRED YEARS)* CONTINUES TO BE HONORED AT MICELI WINE TASTINGS AND GATHERINGS.

Jim Mitchell lived in Paso Robles, California. In the 1990s, he owned a vineyard, produced homemade wine and took courses at Davis and at Cal Poly. In 2002, the former locksmith bought 60 acres on Homedale Road, the old Dakota Vineyard, which he later sold to the ill-fated Polo Cove project. He and his wife, Michele, moved to their Owyhee County riverside home/winery in 2003.

While he no longer has the "big vineyard," he has a small experimental block of about three acres in wine grapes on the banks of the Snake River. He grows zinfandel that he planted in 2005, viognier, tempranillo and he recently added Tablas Creek syrah grapes (from northern California). He also has new plantings of cabernet sauvignon and chardonnay. At around 2,230 feet, the vineyard is lower than those in Canyon County, but he reports that the nights along the river are cold, and getting the grapes ripe can be a challenge. He produces about 240 cases of wine that are sold in Boise, Marsing, and Meridian and are always available in Sunny Slope at the Orchard House.

Ironically, Jim Mitchell didn't "actually get a label until he sold the big vineyard." His philosophy of winemaking is simple: "I just make a wine that we like and hope someone else will." Mitchell has little interest in marketing; he wants "to stay around 500 cases." Miceli began selling its 2005 Cab/Merlot (from the former vineyard) and 2006 Chardonnay (from Symms' vineyards) in 2008. Miceli wines may be homespun, but they've

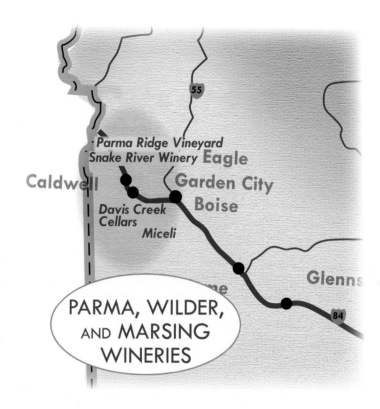

had some recent success in 2009 competitions. The 2006 Cabernet took a bronze at the Treasure Valley Wine Society; it garnered a silver at the Western Idaho State Fair, and his 2006 Zinfandel won a silver at the prestigious Northwest Wine Summit.

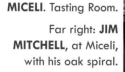

REFRACTOMETER.
Measuring sugars at Miceli.

MICELI. Tasting Room.

Far right: **JIM MITCHELL**, at Miceli, with his oak spiral.

84

BARREL ROOM, boxes. Miceli.

SOUND AND SENSE AND GLASSWARE

When we taste wine we use four of the five senses –taste, smell, touch, sight. "The only one you don't get when you taste wine is sound," says Dick Dickstein. "When  you clink your glasses together, you get the fifth sense." Asked whether glassware makes a difference, he responds, "The big glass gives you a chance to swirl and release oxygen and the esters; half the taste of wine is the aroma." Drinking a big French Bordeaux in a big glass concentrates the wine's flavor. He argues that the new stemless glasses can't help but transfer the heat from your hand to the wine and affect the taste. So next time before you pour, swirl, sniff and taste, be sure to clink first. You will use all your senses.

PARMA RIDGE VINEYARD AND TASTING ROOM

A retired American Airline pilot, Dick Dickstein and his wife Shirley moved to Idaho from Las Vegas in 1997 so he could grow wine grapes. Dickstein selected Idaho because

The land had some Gewürztraminer plants growing along the fence line, so he was pretty sure he could grow grapes. With help from Ste. Chapelle's Chuck Devlin, and using wine grapes from the University of Idaho Parma Extension, they tested 26 grape varietals. Dickstein learned from that 2001 test what would do well, and says, "That's why we have a viognier in Idaho, because it was so good." He maintains that Idaho's "one of the best places in the world to grow viognier."

That same year Dickstein made his first wines. His initial offering was a Merlot, but he wanted to have a white and a red, so he bought some chardonnay grapes. By 2009, he was raising gewürztraminer, merlot, syrah, viognier, chardonnay and some cabernet sauvignon. He is one of the few Idaho grape growers who grows zinfandel, which he describes as "a grape that's the first to bud and last to ripen." But it has done well on

WINEMAKER DICK DICKSTEIN, Parma Ridge Vineyard.

he wanted to raise varietals that didn't grow in Oregon, and his wife did not want to return to her hometown of Walla Walla. Happily, they found their ideal site above the Boise River on Parma Ridge on the first weekend that they went looking. They visited six places on a Friday; the next day they made an offer on their current home and the original vineyard, which had been an orchard. Parma Ridge Vineyard has grown to 12 acres, nine-and-a-half acres in grapes.

his site, where the elevation is about 2,400 feet. Currently, he's crafting a Bordeaux-style wine blend called Mélange with the traditional five varietals—cabernet sauvignon, merlot, petit verdot, malbec and cabernet franc. Some of these varietals he bought from the Wood River Vineyard.

Mélange needs time. It's a long process, Dickstein says, because it takes about three years for the grape plants to yield fruit, a year to ferment. Then the blended wine ages

HARVEST. Parma Ridge Vineyard.

PARMA RIDGE. Harvest.

red varietals are planted in the warmer sections of the vineyard. Dickstein loves to farm and fashion premium vintages but readily admits, "I detest marketing. I would be happy if I could just grow grapes and make wine." That said, Parma Ridge is growing nicely (about 20 percent a year), and the winery has recently redesigned the logo.

in the barrel for a minimum of two years. He's now growing just enough of the varietals to blend his own proprietary Mélange.

Dickstein insists that there's one unyielding fact about growing grapes and making wine, "You'd better like it," because things can, and do, go wrong and then, "it's wait until next year." Not a fan of marketing, he sells most of his wines in his tasting room. He's convinced that Idaho wines are just now being discovered and credits the AVA. "It's helped a lot," he says.

He doesn't "get a big heavy crop" because of his vineyard management; he harvests about two tons to the acre but "the grapes are top quality." His range of vineyard sites allows slower-ripening grapes like gewürztraminer, to be planted on a northeast slope, while the

SNAKE RIVER WINERY AND ARENA VALLEY VINEYARD

Scott and Susan DeSeelhorst own the Snake River Winery and the Arena Valley Vineyard between Parma and Wilder. Scott grew up in Phoenix; his family moved to Salt Lake City in 1989. Skiing has been an essential part of his life for many years. His family owns the Solitude Resort in Utah. Trained as a chef, he continues to spend winters in Utah working at Solitude, where he's in charge of the resort's fine dining operation. His long-term interest in food naturally led to wines and his desire to have a vineyard and a winery.

WINEMAKER SCOTT DeSEELHORST and New Yorker cartoon about Idaho wine.

He and Susan moved up to Boise in 1997, where he says he was "looking for a little ten-acre south-facing place to grow grapes." What they found was something quite different. Originally owned by Norm and Fred Batt, the Arena Valley Vineyard that the DeSeelhorsts bought was planted in 1983 (making it one of the region's oldest) with chardonnay and riesling; cabernet and merlot were added in 1987. Scott and Susan bought the 80-acre vineyard in 1998. The grapes that were growing there then were under contract to Ste. Chapelle through 2000, so the DeSeelhorsts had two years to learn the vineyard business.

Their early winemaking experience was more comic than economic. "We stomped some grapes with our feet and made some really horrible wine," says Scott. They have a photograph to prove it. In 2000, they began to think about where to build a winery; they bought six adjoining acres and built their winery in Arena Valley. Today, they have 76 acres planted in grapes out of their total of 88 acres.

The soil here is "unique," says Scott. The Arena Valley Vineyard faces south and gets a lot of sun. Scott says they can "ripen some of the later-ripening varietals like cabernet and barbera." What makes the Arena Valley special? Scott

SCOTT DeSEELHORST, sampling.

HARVEST. Parma Ridge Vineyard.

SNAKE RIVER WINERY.
Terroir.

states, "The soil is more river sediment and wash, so you have more cobblestone than cinders...very similar to the Rhone Valley."

Scott believes his rocky ground resembles some of the vineyards in and around Walla Walla. He likes to show a photo of Washington's Cayuse Vineyard (an internationally well-known vineyard for syrah) with its cobble-strewn soil and adds, "Cayuse looks just like our vineyard." Scott's first love is "being out in the vineyard." As a grape grower he is "moving toward organic"; currently Snake River farms about 20 acres organically. They harvest from three to four tons per acre. And they can call their riesling and chardonnay plantings "old vines," because the plants are more than 25 years old.

Initially, Snake River produced 500 cases of wine. They actually did an initial foot crush. Soon the winery became fully automated and Snake River made 2,000 cases by 2001. Today Scott describes Snake River as "one of the bigger small wineries," producing between 4,000 to 5,000 cases of diverse varietals and blends. Almost all the wines are done

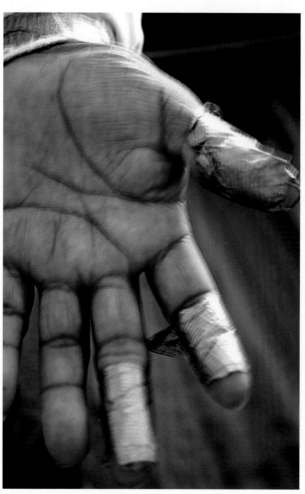

GRAPE PICKER'S PRECAUTION. Tape helps minimize cuts and effects of grape acid.

in small batches. They are growing three of the five port grapes, making a dry red wine from the Portuguese varietal touriga nacional, under the label Touriga. Snake River is also starting to craft a port, done in a traditional style with their Portuguese varietals; it comes out between 18 and 21 percent alcohol. 2015 will be the first vintage.

In 2008, Snake River did a major planting at Arena Valley of malbec, cabernet franc and sangiovese. They are producing more than a dozen wines including Riesling, their biggest production. They do an oaked and unoaked Chardonnay, which "is dramatically different from a barrel-aged Chardonnay," as well as Grenache, Touriga, Tempranillo, Cabernet Sauvignon, and Malbec. Scott DeSeelhorst maintains, "People are talking about the Rhones, but I think malbec is going to be Idaho's grape." When you think about Argentina with its high altitude vineyards and how well the malbec grape does there, it makes sense. Scott adds, "I generally try to do wines that others don't do." To this end he has blocks of blauer zweigelt, grenache and mourvedre.

Even with so many different types of wine grapes, Snake River uses traditional winemaking methods that combine European and American techniques. Scott says, "Our style is what I call old world... we don't use a lot of new oak. We don't make these big fruit-forward wines. And we are strictly using American oak." Recently, he discovered a Virginia oak barrel, which

HARVEST. Snake River Winery.

has "tighter grain that resembles French oak."

Scott sells grapes to other Idaho producers: "It's a cash flow part of the business"; about two thirds of the vineyard is sold to others. The winery has also taken an unusual step

in downtown Boise by establishing Snake River Tasting Room in BoDo, which gives the winery both a marketing presence as well as its largest retail site.

Lately, the company added a second label called

GINA DAVIS ON IDAHO STYLE

I like to say I was trained by Idaho winemakers, who are by no means classically trained. I learned to make wine from Brad Pintler, who was trained as an accountant and he farms... I would say my style is making the best wine possible from the grapes we're getting. We can try to imitate the French or Napa Valley but that might not be best suited to the grapes we get.

WAX. Davis Creek.

Afternoon Wine Company, with wines that sell at a lower price. Scott is especially proud of Snake River's Barbera and the success it has had. But he notes, "I most enjoy making Riesling, because it's good at all stages of the process."

Snake River has won numerous medals and Scott is proud that they've won "concordance golds," which means that all the judges of a given competition selected their vintage for the gold medal. Awards have come from major competitions in San Francisco, Long Beach, Riverside (California) as well as the Indy International and Northwest Wine Summit.

DAVIS CREEK CELLARS

Gina Davis owns and makes the wines for Davis Creek Cellars. Its tasting room resides in a handsome storefront on Main Street in Marsing. The comfortable tasting room combines wine paraphernalia with an ample selection of Davis Creek's production.

Raised on a farm in Sand Hollow, west of Caldwell, she named her winery after Davis Creek near Donnelly where her grandfather farmed. She has made Davis Creek wines on her own terms and in her own style. She spends time among the grapes but believes, "You have to trust the growers." A realist, she understands that a boutique winery may have to wait if a major producer needs the grapes right away.

Considered one of the new wave of creative, young winemakers, Davis learned her profession at some of Idaho's best-known wineries from some of the region's most important winemakers.

A University of Idaho graduate in 2003, she has a degree in horticulture. While in school in Moscow, Davis took several viticulture classes at nearby Washington State University in Pullman and visited Washington vineyards and wineries. Her first job in the wine industry was in the lab at Ste. Chapelle, where she worked with Chuck Devlin and Maureen Johnson. Davis says she learned a lot from Johnson, who is "a quilting buddy who has been in the industry since the Symms owned Ste. Chapelle." Johnson has done extensive training through the University of California at Davis. After that year's harvest and her temporary position ended at Ste. Chapelle, Davis went to work for Sawtooth, where she assisted Brad Pintler (one of Idaho's pioneer vintners and most innovative winemakers).

She stayed there for three years and noticed from the increasing number of people coming to the winery that "the industry was getting to the tipping point that we're at now," so she told herself, "it's now or never and decided to make a deal with Greg Koenig"; she worked in the tasting room with Martin Fujishin—another future winemaker. During the harvest, "I worked seven days a week."

Bolstered by her supportive parents (George and Gayle Davis are fixtures at the Capital City Public Market in Boise, where they pour and sell Davis Creek Cellars wines), she contacted Dennis McArthur, who then owned the Wood River Vineyard, to buy malbec and some tempranillo. She also sourced grapes from Skyline and from a vineyard in Washington and bought some tempranillo from Windy Ridge Vineyard in Kuna.

Her initial production went from 600 in 2007 to 1,100 cases in 2008. She does about a dozen hand-crafted wines in small batches. Her wines include Malbec, Tempranillo, Syrah, Cabernet Sauvignon, Pinot Grigio, Merlot, Late Harvest Syrah and Viognier. She says, "To be able to get locally grown wine grapes that

WINEMAKER Gina Davis.

are the French and Spanish grapes has been huge."

She puts her reds through malolactic (secondary) fermentation and she uses a fair amount of used oak barrels that she believes are "a little bit milder and a little bit more approachable." She adds, in Idaho "as an industry where we cannot afford to use new oak, we have to make some decisions based on the bottom line. For me, it hasn't been a problem because of the flavor profile I am going for." Blending seems to come naturally to this experimental winemaker. Her South Mountain Red—a blend of tempranillo, touriga nacional, malbec, petit verdot with 50 percent cabernet—got its name from a mountain in the Owyhees on the Idaho side, but only accessible from Oregon. It too sold out quickly.

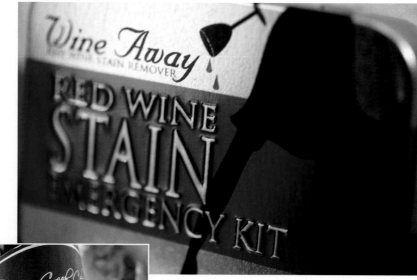

DAVIS CREEK. Label. Stain emergency kit.

Davis Creek Cellars Malbec won a double gold and her Tempranillo, a single gold, at the 2009 Northwest Wine Summit. The awards were gratifying but not surprising; she says, "We were about sold out already, I guess our customers knew already." For now, she plans to "hold steady right around a thousand cases." Davis Creek Cellars has many repeat customers and a wine club; recently she's moved her winemaking operations to the University of Idaho Incubator site on Chicago Street in Caldwell.

The aesthetics of Davis Creek Cellars matter. From the distinctive gray labels, which Tammy Stowe designed, to the wax she uses to cap her bottles, Gina Davis makes thoughtful decisions.

BOISE CO-OP. Danielle DeMeester.

FRASER WINERY AND VINEYARD. Harvest.

HELLS CANYON. Crush. Bijou Robertson, right, and company.

Microclimate, Sawtooth Vineyards

CHAPTER FIVE

NAMPA

SAWTOOTH WINERY, SAWTOOTH AND SKYLINE VINEYARDS

N AMPA-BASED SAWTOOTH WINERY OCCUPIES A

UNIQUE PLACE IN THE IDAHO WINE INDUSTRY. SAWTOOTH BOTH PRO-

DUCES AWARD-WINNING PREMIUM WINES UNDER THEIR OWN LABELS

FROM THEIR OWN GRAPES AND OWNS AND OPERATES TWO OF THE

STATE'S LARGEST AND MOST IMPORTANT VINEYARDS, SAWTOOTH AND

SKYLINE. THE SAWTOOTH VINEYARDS SUPPLY MOST OF THE GRAPES

FOR STE. CHAPELLE, AS WELL AS ITS OWN BRANDS AND MANY SMALLER

PRODUCERS. THEIR VINEYARDS HAVE ALSO PRODUCED SOME OF THE

MOST UNUSUAL VINIFERA IN THE GEM STATE.

Originally founded as Pintler Cellars by pioneer vintner Brad
Pintler, the Sawtooth Winery and Tasting Room sits on top of a
beautiful sloping vineyard above the Snake River. The two vineyards
combined are by far the state's largest plantings of wine grapes.
Corus Brands, Sawtooth's parent company, now owns 540 of the
state's roughly 1600 acres of vineyards. Skyline, the newer and
larger vineyard, has south, east, west and north-facing slopes that

101

SAWTOOTH VINEYARDS. Summer.

present unique microclimates and allows for great wine grape experimentation. The University of Idaho Research extension in Parma leases an experimental block here as well. Sawtooth represents one of the warmer sites in southwest Idaho; cabernet sauvignon ripens here and the vineyards produce cabernet franc, malbec, roussanne, pinot gris, syrah and merlot, among others.

Recently, Napa, California native Bill Murray took over as the winemaker at Sawtooth. Murray has been in the industry since 1988. In California, he worked briefly at Buena Vista, then spent 13 years at Acacia, first as cellar master then vineyard manager. In 2002, he went with winemaker Michael Richmond to work at first as an enologist and then ran the winemaking operation as associate winemaker at Bouchaine Vineyards. Why Sawtooth? Murray says, "I came to a point in my life where I wanted to make wine in a different area." Idaho beckoned.

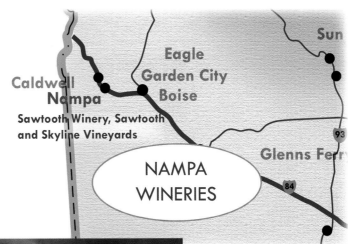

SKYLINE VINEYARDS. Mechanical harvester. Dawn.

Sawtooth makes about 10,000 cases a year. Murray, whose background focused on pinot noir, is excited about the Rhone varietals, but readily adds, "I fell in love with the tempranillo." He states, "We will continue to make what Sawtooth has done well—the Cabernet, the Merlot and the Syrah." Sawtooth's vineyards are evolving. They are removing some varietals that struggle here and adding more pinot gris. But Murray has been impressed with Sawtooth's production. He credits Brad Pintler, who he says, "has done an outstanding job making wines to represent the region."

In January of 2009, he became winemaker at Sawtooth, where he oversees the state's second largest winery. A skier, marathon runner, tri-athlete and Iron Man participant, southwest Idaho made sense. He has also lived in Europe, which he says "spawned my interest in wine," and spent time in Oregon and Washington but decided that the Boise area was his "number one choice," because of the physical attributes and the potential of the wine region. Murray realizes that he's replacing a legend in Brad Pintler, but sees Idaho winemaking as an extraordinary opportunity.

One significant change that the brand recently undertook is adopting a new label and look. Their iconic jagged-peak (freeform) labels have been replaced by a more traditional-looking image of the Sawtooths set inside a rectangular label. Assistant winemaker Mike Crowley (who

is also the winemaker and owner of Syringa) believes that the new labels "are more sophisticated."

Sawtooth's vineyards continue to grow an array of distinctive varietals, including muscat blanc, petit verdot and a small amount of primitivo (an Italian grape that is related to zinfandel). Even though some varietals like cabernet franc, semillon and cabernet sauvignon are being ripped out, more tempranillo is being planted; in a few years its production will increase substantially. This classic Spanish varietal "sits somewhere between pinot noir and cabernet. Tempranillo is a wine that's not real light but not too big, that's sweet in the palate, " says Murray, and it offers "hints of tobacco and berry flavors."

The 2009 harvest surprised Sawtooth. Some blocks produced as much as six to seven tons of grapes to the acre. Murray says, "We didn't expect that." Asked what stood out in his first year at Sawtooth, he notes some distinct differences in the way grapes grow in Idaho as compared to California. He points out that in California the sugars rise more quickly and the fruit characteristics follow; in Idaho he sees the opposite. "The fruit tastes ripen first but the sugar is not quite there yet."

Sawtooth will continue to produce a large quantity of riesling (traditionally a grape that's done well in the region); their crop was up by more than 15 percent this year. Sawtooth makes a sweet Riesling (4,000-plus cases) and a dry (500 to 800 cases). The winery crafts a variety of wines. In 2009, Sawtooth sold 18 different wines, but Murray looks to "condense" that number, and adds pragmatically, "We must make sure that we sell all the wine we make."

Sawtooth's well-equipped tasting room and landscaped grounds create one of the regions most used venues for tastings and parties. The variety of vintages to sample and grand views make it one of Idaho wine country's most memorable stops.

DAWN. Sawtooth Winery. Receiving harvest.

An INTERVIEW with KEN MCCABE

President, Corus Estates & Vineyards

What plans do you have for Sawtooth?
Our plan is to be the winery in Idaho that would produce the best quality wine. We have upgraded the winery with state-of-the-art equipment and with Bill Murray now there, we should be able to create this vision.

Do you expect to expand the market for your wines?
Yes. We are currently in 24 states, but would like to add 10 more in 2010. We don't want to be everywhere, and we certainly want to be selling Sawtooth in the areas that people want to try great wines from the Northwest, but not particularly from Washington or Oregon.

What varietals do you plan to concentrate on?
Currently, we focus on syrah, chardonnay, and riesling, but we have planted a lot more tempranillo and malbec grapes. We feel those will be the future of Sawtooth and Idaho.

What are your thoughts about Idaho as a place to grow grapes and as a destination for wine tourism?
I think Idaho is an ideal place to grow grapes. It has been an agricultural state for years, so the climate is good for vinifera grapes. The high elevation (around 3,000 feet above sea level) also helps with grape growing. We have long days, so we get that great natural acidity and balance. We have had a lot more good years than off years in Idaho.

ORIGINAL LABEL.

Where does Sawtooth fit in your company's brands?

We produce estate wines from the three Northwest states, and Sawtooth is an integral part of the overall company vision. We have diversity in all three states, and I feel some wines will produce better in Idaho than the other two states. People are always pleasantly surprised when they try Sawtooth for the first time. It is usually the consumer's first time trying an Idaho wine.

How do you see Sawtooth's role in the Idaho wine industry since you are both a major wine producer and own and manage the largest vineyards?

We will always have a major role in the Idaho wine industry. Our vineyards have been there for almost as long as the industry, so people look to us for advice and opinions. It has been fun to learn and to have others in the industry learn with us. The Idaho wine industry is comparable to Washington in the late 1980s, but we are catching up fast and I think you will see world-class wines coming out of Idaho in the next five years.

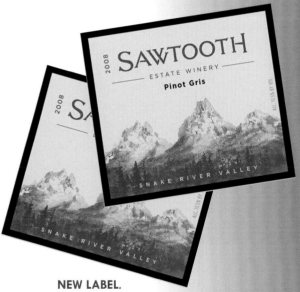

NEW LABEL.

"We have long days, so we get that great natural acidity and balance."

~ Ken McCabe

107

IRRIGATION. Cold Springs Winery.

IRRIGATION.

Picker with bandanna. Cinder.

CHAPTER SIX

GARDEN CITY AND BOISE

M CINDER

ELANIE KRAUSE, CO-OWNER WITH HER HUSBAND JOE SCHNERR, MAKES CINDER'S WINES IN A UTILITARIAN WAREHOUSE IN GARDEN CITY. A BOISE NATIVE, SHE STUDIED BIOLOGY AT WASHINGTON STATE, SPEAKS SPANISH," WHICH HELPS IN THE VINE- YARDS," TAUGHT ENGLISH IN CHINA AND, MOST IMPORTANTLY, WORKED FOR FIVE YEARS AT CHATEAU STE. MICHELLE'S CANOE RIDGE ESTATE WINERY IN WASHINGTON FOCUSING ON RED WINES. AT CHATEAU STE. MICHELLE, SHE STARTED IN THE VINEYARDS AND ENDED UP AS AS- SISTANT WINEMAKER AT A FACILITY THAT PRODUCED A PRODIGIOUS 400,000 CASES PER YEAR.

She wanted to return to Idaho and began scoping out the Idaho vineyards. In 2006, she came home and did some wine consulting and thoroughly studied the local vineyards. She's committed to local vintners. "I am buying all my grapes in Idaho. I totally believe this area can produce world-class wines." She chooses her Viognier from three different vineyards and uses up to six different yeasts. These days, Cinder buys grapes from six different vineyards and contracts "specific rows in the vineyard." She's also very specific in her instructions; she prefers to have heavier crop (about four tons per acre), and to have the grapes picked earlier for her Rosé of Syrah than her Syrah, so there are fewer tannins and lower alcohol.

In 2008, Cinder began with 350 cases divided among Viognier, Rosé and Syrah, which sold out. In 2009, she released a thousand cases; this year she plans to release 1,400 cases of five different wines. Her varietals come from Williamson, whose grapes produce wines that have "a lot of body and backbone," Skyline, where the grapes

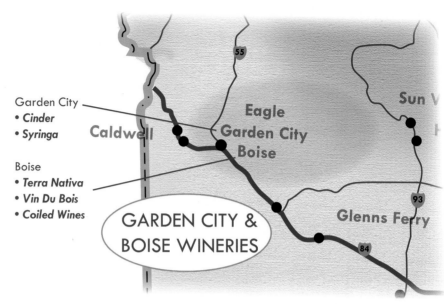

Garden City
• *Cinder*
• *Syringa*

Boise
• *Terra Nativa*
• *Vin Du Bois*
• *Coiled Wines*

GARDEN CITY & BOISE WINERIES

produce "more aromatic but lighter-bodied wines," and Sawtooth, which is the "complete package" full-bodied and aromatic. She's also gotten grapes from Emmett's Rocky Fence

Vineyard. "It's a tiny vineyard. He doesn't have a lot planted. I only got one barrel of Viognier and two of Tempranillo but they're so good." She likes Idaho's sandy loam soil with its basalt layers—and cinder. She named her wine as a tribute to this volcanic component in the region's soils.

Currently an Idaho Grape Growers and Wine Commission member, Krause has made an immediate impact in Idaho's wine world. Cinder has admirers statewide. She enjoys discussing varietals and their characteristics: "Malbec's a really vigorous vine that has lots of potential here, can be planted in more depleted soils; syrah's adaptable." The famous Rhone varietal does well in Idaho and Washing-

Left: **CINDER.** Chardonnay wine.
MELANIE KRAUSE. Winemaker, Cinder.

112

ton. She loves wines in the Rhone-style and says, "I really like Washington-style wines because I learned to make wine there…but mostly I like wines that are well balanced."

SYRINGA

Winemaker Mike Crowley has a double life in winemaking. He works as the assistant winemaker at Sawtooth and the owner/winemaker for his own brand, Syringa. Crowley recently relocated his winemaking operation and tasting room to Chinden Boulevard in Garden City.

Crowley began working in the industry in 2000. He went through the viticulture and enology program at Walla Walla Community College, did additional schooling at WSU and has a degree in Production Management (BBA) from Boise State University. He put in three years at Walla Walla Vintners, a winery that specializes in premium reds, before coming to work at Sawtooth.

Syringa (Idaho's state flower) is named after his niece. Crowley began making wine in 2002 and dates his own brand to 2004; his first wines were released in 2009. His first wine was a 2004 Merlot; he also does Cabernet, Primitivo, Sauvignon Blanc (that's off dry) and Malbec. He began at around 500 cases and wants to level off at about a 1,000. He sources his grapes mostly from the Snake River Valley but has sourced some from Washington as well.

Dedicated to traditional labor-intensive methods including frequent visits to the vineyard, Crowley uses only hand-picked and hand-sorted grapes for his wines—

WINEMAKER MIKE CROWLEY. Syringa.

methods that he believes "are gentler on the grapes." He outlines the essence of his winemaking philosophy on his website: wines are unfiltered… and cellared in separate vineyard lots in American, French, and Hungarian oak barrels. The "free run" [unprocessed juice] and "pressed wines" are placed in separate barrels for aging, and then later blended by [winemakers with] discerning palates.

Crowley embraces the Urban Wine Cooperative concept of "three separate wineries under one roof, sharing resources and knowledge and building Idaho's wine industry." He recognizes that the Idaho wine industry is evolving. Syringa's one of the few wineries in Idaho that makes Primitivo, an earthy wine that pairs well with barbecue. Surprisingly, he notes, "People who like my Primitivo don't seem to like the Merlot and those who like the Merlot don't seem to like the Primitivo." Crowley's Primitivo comes from the Sawtooth Vineyard.

His goal is to make consistent, high-quality wines. Crowley worked under Brad Pintler and credits Pintler's influence on Idaho's industry. He says, "Pintler has been a huge asset to the wine industry and the growth and reputation of the valley. He showed me how to expand my premium red wines [as well as] some techniques to balance out my white wines."

Syringa wants to have its own unique place in Idaho's wine world. Crowley says, "I don't want to have the same wines as John and Melanie at the Cooperative and I chose Sauvignon Blanc and Primitivo, [because] I don't believe anyone else is producing them in the state."

WINEMAKERS Dick Pavelek (left) and Tim Day (right). Terra Nativa.

TERRA NATIVA

Owned by Dick Pavelek and Tim Day, Terra Nativa is a five-acre vineyard that sits hidden in a cul-de-sac above the old Idaho Penitentiary and is the focal point of a unique Boise housing development. "The subdivision worked because people enjoy living around a vineyard." Day says. Terra Nativa's also the brand of one of Idaho's newer vintages. Grapes were planted in the late 1990s, and they first bottled their wine in 2002. Pavelek credits vintner Cheyne Weston who he says, "has been extremely helpful." For the first several years Terra Nativa crushed, fermented and aged their wines at Weston's facility in Sunny Slope.

Terra Nativa recently moved their cellar operation to a 1913 building at 136 East Idaho Street in Meridian, where they barrel-age the wine. Ultimately, there will be a tasting room by appointment in the wine cellar in Meridian. They grow syrah, merlot, malbec, cabernet sauvignon and cabernet franc as well as some whites—semillon and pinot gris. They aim to produce mostly blended, Bordeaux-style, wines. The vineyard can produce between 20 and 22 tons of grapes. Pavelek and Day agree that this former pear orchard provides an exceptional site to grow grapes. They are fortunate because the site has good air drainage, a variety of soil groups, and soil that is suitable to grow wine grapes.

It has "four to six feet of clay on top of the sand" and therefore has a rich mineral content. Pavelek, a landscape architect who lives by the vineyard, says, "it has kind of deep, hard soil," so it "allows us to ripen fruit that wouldn't normally ripen in this location." Day adds, "This is the only commercial vineyard within the Boise City limits."

Terra Nativa plans to produce between 800 and 1,000 cases a year. They make five reds—Merlot, Petit Syrah, Malbec, Cabernet Franc and Cabernet Sauvignon. Their plants are a decade old, and they are located on a "perched water table," says Day. This setting "accumulates the miner-

als in the water. And that will allow us to make some quality wines."

Asked where he believes his wines and Idaho wines generally fit, Pavelek says, "Our fruit can't hang on the vines so long [as in California], and our grapes are raised more for fruit than pristine wine flavors [as in Europe]. By necessity of climate we'll [have the flavor of] an interior Northwest wine flavor." Like Sunny Slope, the Terra Nativa Vineyard benefits from long, sunny days and cool, dry nights. The owners planted in 1999, 2000, and 2002 and use only their own grapes. Their grapes typically reach about 28 brix of sugar, are drip-irrigated and picked by hand.

TERRA NATIVA. Dawn, with Table Rock, Boise, at rear.

Their location has had its challenges, Pavelek says, "The first year we harvested, we lost all of our merlot to two big bucks, mule deer." Coyotes also seem to like the grapes; "there are 20 to 30 of them" who have been regularly chased away. For grape-loving birds they've come up with a unique method to protect the vines. They use a sound system, "an electronic scarecrow" of piped-in predator sounds to scare away the birds that are attracted to the grapes.

VIN DU BOIS

Ted Judd loves the world of wine. He's promoted wine tastings, competitions, organizations and he's been an itinerant winemaker, making his vintages in Kuna, Parma and Boise. Soon, he plans to settle and open a winery and tasting room in a multi-tenanted winery that Lloyd Mahaffey is developing in Eagle.

His path to winemaking evolved from his travels and his experience going to Canyon County during harvest, watching the crush and witnessing the process of crafting wines. Twenty-five years ago, the Pocatello native began traveling and tasting wines in earnest. His influence on the local industry comes from his passion for wines. Judd helped found the Treasure Valley Wine Society, a chapter of the Enological Society of the Pacific Northwest. In 2000, he helped organize the first tasting event (Pinot Noirs) and four years later helped initiate the Idaho Wine Festival.

Judd's been experimenting, making his own wine and

BOISE CO-OP. The store offers a wide variety of wines.

helping others since the 1990s. He released his first commercial wine in 2006. He has made a Pinot Noir, an unoaked Chardonnay, Pinot Gris and a blend called Enigma, which he describes as "equal parts syrah, souzo, touriga nacional, and malbec with brandy made from cabernet… " under the Les Bois label. Currently, he's producing Pinot Gris, Chardonnay, Merlot, Cabernet, Malbec, and a blend of the reds for Vin du Bois with, as his label says, "a little help from my friends."

COILED WINES

Leslie Preston, a Napa Valley resident but Boise native, crafted Idaho's newest wine. The Coiled label, inspired by the Snake River Valley AVA, produces wines made exclusively from Idaho grapes. Currently, Preston is focusing all her attention on the syrah grape, as she considers it to be one of Idaho's most promising varietals. She has impressive California wine country credentials. Preston earned an M.S. in Enology from Davis. She says on her website, "My professional training includes time at Clos du Bois, in Sonoma, and Saintsbury in Carneros, before landing a dream job at Stags' Leap Winery in the Stags Leap District of the Napa Valley."

When the time came to start her own label, she decided to become part of her home state's wine industry and created her own all-Idaho wine from Sawtooth and Skyline Vineyards; she made the wine at Fraser's Winery in Boise and aged and bottled it in St. Helena, California. Preston says, "Coiled celebrates the promise of Idaho's first grape-growing appellation, the Snake River Valley, which winds its way through southwestern Idaho." A highly informed wine-maker, she deliberately chose screw caps because "there is simply nothing more disappointing than a well-made wine ruined by cork taint." She made 300 cases of 2008 Snake River Valley Coiled Syrah, which debuted in November of 2009 with tastings at Fraser's in Boise and at the New Vintage Wine Shop in Meridian.

The Boise Co-op's wine aficionado David Kirkpatrick wrote in *Boise Co-op Uncorked* January 2010, "Coiled's 2008 is everything you want in a red wine…. Really shows the potential of Syrah here in our home state."

COILED WINE at Boise Co-op.

"Coiled's 2008 is everything you want in a red wine…. Really shows the potential of Syrah here in our home state."

David Kirkpatrick
Boise Co-op

BITNER VINEYARDS. Looking South.

SNAKE RIVER WINERY. Harvest. Dawn.

120

SNAKE RIVER WINERY. Harvest.

WILLIAMSON. Pre-pruning.

PREPARING FOR HARVEST. Dawn. Snake River Winery.

Bill Stowe and company, Indian Creek.

CHAPTER SEVEN

KUNA

INDIAN CREEK

DUBBED THE GODFATHER OF IDAHO WINE INDUSTRY, BILL STOWE, THE FOUNDER AND LONGTIME WINEMAKER AT INDIAN CREEK, HAS INFLUENCED SOME OF THE STATE'S MOST SIGNIFICANT VINTNERS AND GRAPE GROWERS. BRAD PINTLER AND GREG KOENIG, TWO OF THE INDUSTRY'S MOST IMPORTANT VINTNERS, BOTH WORKED AT INDIAN CREEK. NOW STOWE'S DAUGHTER TAMMY AND SON-IN-LAW MIKE MCCLURE ARE BENEFITING FROM STOWE'S STEWARDSHIP AND KNOWLEDGE.

An Idaho native and Air Force veteran, Stowe traces his interest in grape growing and winemaking to a stint in Germany. There he learned about the art of creating handcrafted wines while in the service. He even worked a couple of crushes, and the seeds were sown for his passionate pursuit of making wines in his home state.

In the 1980s, Bill and his wife Mui bought more than 20 acres in Kuna while he was stationed at Mountain Home Air Force Base. As the story goes, he drove the same red International Harvester tractor that he still rides up from Mountain Home to his vineyard near Indian Creek. That was a quarter of a century ago.

Stowe's admirers say he could grow grapes on a slab of stone, and his vineyard in Kuna is one of the oldest and best established in southwest Idaho. He readily admits that Kuna may not be the warmest spot in the valley, but points out that the climate and limestone-laden soil has been more than hospitable to wine grapes.

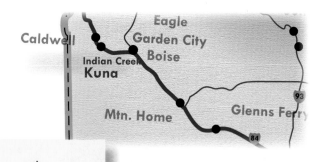

Growing pinot noir grapes made his early reputation. A notoriously difficult varietal that thrives in Oregon's moist Willamette Valley—and was famously touted on film in *Sideways* —Stowe's Indian Creek Pinot Noirs won major accolades from the outset. His 1988 Pinot Noir took the best red wine award (out of 889 entries) from the San Diego National Wine Competition in 1990.

Stowe founded the winery with his brother Mike and Rich Ostrogorsky. Mike Stowe taught school and took wine classes in America's academic wine capital, Davis, California. They planted grapes in the mid-eighties but suffered a killing frost in the winter of 1985-86, so the winery dates to 1987. A man of weaker constitution might have packed in his dream of making wine in Kuna after frosts nearly destroyed three of the first five crops, but Bill Stowe persevered. The next 20 years the weather cooperated, and Indian Creek now produces almost five thousand cases of about a dozen wines.

At elevation 2,626, this high-altitude vineyard and winery produces a rich palate of varietals and blends. Red wines

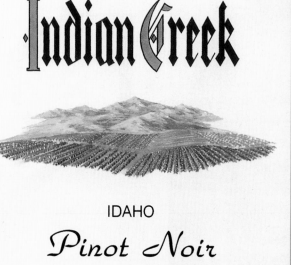

IDAHO

Pinot Noir

1988

offered include Syrah, Pinot Noir, Malbec, Star Garnet, Cabernet, and Ruby Port and white wines include Chardonnay, Mountain Syringa, White Riesling, the unique white Pinot Noir and a Rosé.

Winepress Northwest named Indian Creek Idaho Winery of the Year in 2008. Stowe and family continue to innovate; last year they produced a small batch of 100 percent Petit Verdot.

Stowe, now in his 70s, recently turned the family business over to his daughter and son-in-law. Daughter Tammy designs wine labels, takes care of the website and manages events (weddings are popular), and her husband Mike became the winemaker. Everyone still works the soil and the vines.

Bill's still around, riding his tractor, dispensing wisdom and sharing Idaho wine lore.

POST BUD BREAK.

BITNER (right in distance) **AND SYMMS VINEYARDS** (foreground). Winter.

ROSES. Early pest detectors. Netting. Protection from hungry birds.

Spring pruning. 3 Horse Ranch Vineyards.

CHAPTER EIGHT

EAGLE AND WEISER

O *PÉRIPLE*

RIGINALLY FROM BOISE, ANGIE RIFF GRADUATED FROM THE UNIVERSITY OF IDAHO IN 1999, WHERE SHE STUDIED MICROBIOLOGY, MOLECULAR BIOLOGY, AND BIOCHEMISTRY. SHE MOVED TO SONOMA AND DECIDED THAT SHE COULD EITHER PURSUE AN ADVANCED DEGREE IN ENOLOGY AT DAVIS OR LEARN TO MAKE WINE ON THE JOB. SHE FOLLOWED HER HEART; HER CAREER PATH INCLUDES WORKING ON TWO HARVESTS AT ALEXANDER VALLEY VINEYARDS AND, MOST IMPORTANTLY, APPRENTICING WITH, THEN ASSISTING, HELEN TURLEY, THE LEGENDARY CALIFORNIA WINEMAKER.

BRIX. 3 Horse Ranch.

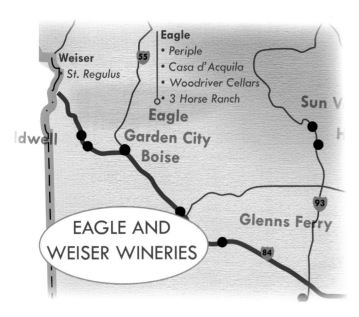

EAGLE AND
WEISER WINERIES

She worked for Turley for four years, ultimately as cellar master/ assistant winemaker on Turley's own label at Marcassin Wine Company. Riff writes on her website:

> Throughout the four years working for Helen, no winery task was left unturned from cleaning tanks, to orchestrating harvest and bottling—all critical to the function of a small winery.

Although Riff's primary role was in the winery, keeping a hand in and having an understanding of the vineyard was mandatory in learning to make great wine. Angie Riff is the Périple winemaker.

The French word Périple translates as spiritual journey; there's a labyrinth on the label that symbolizes the process of winemaking, as well as the literal journey the grapes make and her journey as a winemaker. She uses grapes from Napa Valley that are crushed in California. Then the juice is trucked to Idaho, where she cellars and ages her Pinot Noir in Garden City.

PÉRIPLE. Angie Riff.

Currently, this interstate operation produces about 400 cases of Syrah and Pinot Noir; ultimately she plans to expand to 1,000 cases and do a Chardonnay. She says, "What's interesting about Idaho is I have the chance to make wine from four different states because everything is accessible. So the label will encompass California, Washington, Oregon and eventually Idaho."

Périple has an unusual marketing strategy because "it's meant to be a mailing list brand," Riff says. Eighty percent of the sales will come from the mailing list and about 20 percent from restaurants. "The idea is to create more demand than you can meet."

Why Pinot Noir? The varietal is Angie Riff's passion. "It's a wine for any season, that is elegant [and] can be taken in many directions in terms of style. It's difficult to farm and expensive to make." The winemaker can "hit all the flavor points from one grape," she adds. The film *Sideways* increased demand too. The Périple Pinot Noir is made from 100 percent pinot noir grapes; she favors those from the Russian River region. She notes her 2008 was more Burgundian in style and the 2009 more Californian. She chose Idaho because "I can have the best of both worlds, can live here and make the wine I love."

CASA D'ACQUILA

Angie Riff's business partner, Lloyd Mahaffey, owns Dynamis Group. He has developed a vineyard estate concept, manages vineyards and is soon opening a multi-tenanted winery facility in Eagle. When he moved to his vineyard/home/estate in Eagle, he had the soil tested locally. Surprised at the results, he had the soil retested in California—and the results were the same. Mahaffey's ground is an outstanding terrain to raise wine grapes; he's growing

sangiovese on his own estate vineyard in Eagle. These are some of the area's most fastidiously tended wines.

Riff will be the winemaker for his soon-to-be-released Casa d'Acquila wines. Mahaffey was instrumental in developing the Eagle Wine District, the first of its kind in Idaho. Included in the Eagle Foothills Comprehensive Plan, the wine district insures that cell towers are hidden, allows for more vineyard acreage and lower berms to let in sunlight. Mahaffey is also one of the proponents of the Idaho Viticulture Research Center. A partnership with Boise State University and the College of Western Idaho, this multi-tenanted facility will allow wine to be processed, marketed, and distributed. Viticulture courses will be taught. The wine distribution center and tasting room facility is slated to be built in Eagle.

Mahaffey clearly understands that marketing of Idaho wines takes vision and believes his wine estates and vineyard management fit the industry's future and Eagle's place in it. Eagle is not just a good area for viticulture (on about the same latitude as Tuscany), but "it's where the buyers are," he says. By 2020, he believes Eagle should have upwards of 20 vineyards. In his Vigne d'Acquila (Italian for vines of Eagle) subdivision, each house has a vineyard. And Mahaffey's vineyard management operation is helping to make his prediction come true. The company manages several vineyards in addition to Mahaffey's.

WOODRIVER CELLARS

Dave and Karen Buich bought the former Eagle Knoll winery as well as the Woodriver Vineyard in Wilder. The Buichs have rebranded the wine, upgraded and expanded the facilities at the winery and event center located near Eagle. One of their first decisions was to employ local

WOODRIVER CELLARS. Chardonnay crush.

winemaker Neil Glancey to supervise grape-growing as well as winemaking operations.

The Woodriver Vineyard in Wilder has produced award-winning wines for 15 years. Known for its malbec, used by Pend d'Oreille and Davis Creek among others, this vineyard gives Woodriver Cellars access to some of the AVA's best fruit. With 26 (of 30) acres in vines, the vineyard also produces petit verdot, cabernet sauvignon and merlot. According to Glancey, Woodriver Cellars is set up "to do Bordeaux- style red blends." Their Cab/Malbec contains 40 percent malbec. Their Meritage will make ample use of these well-established vines. This vineyard has just the right soil and setting for malbec, a grape that does poorly in moist climates and thrives in this dry, warm site. They plan to do about "30 tons of malbec" (about 2,400 cases a year), 1,200 cases of Meritage, 600 cases of Chardonnay and about 800 cases of Riesling from Snake River's Arena Valley Vineyard. For now, they produce around 5,000 cases.

A Boise native, Glancey worked with his dad in the ethanol business, then moved to Florida where he first worked in fine dining. The viticulture bug bit him while he was in Florida, and he learned to make wine at Lakeridge and San Sebastian Wineries. Lakeridge produces 55,000 cases per annum and is the Sunshine state's largest winery.

Glancey owns a 10-acre vineyard in King Hill, where he grows merlot with plans to add blocks of gewürztraminer and zinfandel. He used to be the winemaker and general manager at Carmela, but came to Woodriver to focus on wine-making. Glancey is getting a lot of support from the owners, who have upgraded equipment. He now uses "new French oak barrels," and adds, "I am able to control the grapes from start to finish." He's convinced that Woodriver Vineyard at 2,300 feet—lower and warmer than many other sites in the Snake River Valley AVA—will continue to yield great fruit. Reds will become their signature.

This winemaker knows the vagaries of growing grapes from

WOODRIVER CELLARS.

SPRING CLIMATE.

his own experience. A season back, a hailstorm destroyed Glancey's King Hill crop. He maintains that dry cold winters actually harm the vines more than heavy, wet winters because the plants don't get as cold. He's restructuring the vineyards around the winery in Eagle, pulling out varietals that didn't thrive in the site. Glancey plans to add semillon or chardonnay, both relatively early-ripeners, at the Woodriver Canyon Winery vineyard.

Change is afoot at the winery. Woodriver Cellars Winery has moved the Tasting Room into the Barrel Room; the rebranding of the wines and the winery began with the name change in the summer of 2008. Kristin Dudley designed the distinctive label with the meandering river. The event center and grounds have become an important entertainment venue. Originally planned as the centerpiece of a housing development, the winery has moved into con-

certs, weddings and other events. Future plans include hotel rooms, expanded picnic grounds and perhaps a restaurant.

As Woodriver Cellars redefines its venue and reinvents its brand, the wines are already making their mark, winning awards and being added to restaurant menus.

3 HORSE RANCH VINEYARDS

3 Horse Ranch owners Gary and Martha Cunningham live about 12 miles west of Eagle in a secluded valley, where they have about 50 horses and raise certified organic, premium wine grapes. Their vineyards, their business model, their wines (crafted by the ubiquitous Greg Koenig) have taken the Idaho wine industry by storm.

The Cunninghams lived in McCall for almost eight years. They bought the ranch in 1998 and began planting vineyards and doing the "vineyard project" in 2002. They have had as many as 134 horses on the 1,600 acres, but growing organic vinifera in this unique area is their passion. Currently, they have 30 acres in vineyard. Martha says, "We think the ranch is capable of supporting about 400 acres in vines; our

Above: **3 HORSE RANCH.**

Left: **3 HORSE RANCH** on ice.

goal is to produce 100 percent estate-grown, organically-certified wines and we are well on our way. We do have to make some of our wines from other Snake River Valley AVA grapes, because some of our vines are not mature enough." Eventually, they will grow all the grapes for their wines. The grapes are handpicked and sorted at 3 Horse and then sent to Greg Koenig's facility for crushing, fermenting and finishing. "They ultimately return in a bottle," Martha notes.

3 Horse Ranch has planted an impressive mix of varietals from some highly pedigreed rootstocks. "We started off planting one- and two-acre test blocks… and weren't disappointed in any of the grapes," says Gary. He adds, "We have planted some historic rootstock that dates back to Château de Beaucastel in the 1700s." These grapes are classic southern Rhone varietals, and their tests are telling the Cunninghams that "this ground and Idaho has

3 HORSE RANCH.

the capacity for a lot of Rhone varietals": grenache, mourvedre, syrah, viognier and roussanne.

Gary Cunningham and 3 Horse are blazing their own trail. 3 Horse Ranch Vineyards is the first in Idaho to bottle and release a 100 percent Roussanne and a 50/50 Roussanne and Viognier blend. Gary says, "We are primarily going to focus in the future on planting the southern Rhone varietals." In 2009, they planted almost six acres in sauvignon blanc, a late-budding and early-ripening grape, so "selecting the ground was tricky," Gary says. But 3 Horse found just the place for this varietal.

PREP. 3 Horse Ranch.

As impressive as the grape-growing effort has been, 3 Horse has done an inspired job of marketing and branding. Their production has grown exponentially. Initially, they produced around 500 cases; in 2008, that number grew to 5,000; today, the winery produces about 10,000 cases and the goal, Martha says, "is to be just under 20,000 cases." 3 Horse's success and growth surprised both Gary and Martha. The reaction to 3 Horse has been remarkably good. They've won medals in Idaho, San Francisco, Indiana and at the Northwest Wine Summit.

Their planting philosophy is to create a wine in which "we can taste our terroir" Gary says. They are "the first to produce an award-winning wine from the foothills of Eagle," he adds. The vineyard's management matters to them. They decided to become an organic winery, according to Martha "because we live here."

The vineyards slope from north to south and sit at elevations from 2,800 at the road rising to 2,950 feet at the house. Depending on the varietal, 3 Horse Ranch Vineyards average about four tons to the acre. The Cunninghams prune and crop to a smaller yield to produce better wine. They utilize deficit irrigation and "one of the advantages is we are a state-of-the-art vineyard...we do everything by drip irrigation," Gary says. He believes that if "you produce good quality fruit, you are going to produce good wine." He's spent "seven or eight years, totally submerged in the wine world... you learn a lot by doing." Gary insists that Idaho has to evolve from producing in quantity to making quality wines. Long term, they plan to have a winery and production facility on site. Recently, they built a tasting room at the ranch.

Both are realists and understand it takes time to prove how good the vineyards are. Gary thinks, "From 2009 to 2115, you are going to see an enormous change in Idaho wine industry," and he expresses a definite opinion about how Idaho winemaking should progress. While he accepts that wineries in the north and elsewhere source their fruit from Washington, Oregon and California, he's convinced the future of the industry and especially the AVA must be in southwest Idaho. "I think that we will never have an Idaho wine industry until the consumer believes that we are producing Idaho wines from Idaho grapes. If we are going to grow as an industry, we are going to have to use Snake River Valley fruit."

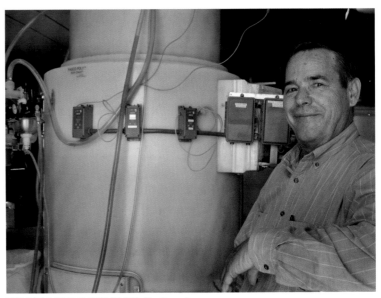

WINEMAKER DAVE RULE. St. Regulus.

ST. REGULUS UNIQUE WINES

Dave and Judy Rule own one of the state's newest and most unusual wineries, St. Regulus. The name derives from an 11th-century medieval tower in Scotland that's called St. Regulus or St. Rule. The Rules describe St. Regulus Wines as "old-world tradition with state-of-the-art methods." Located just outside Weiser, the winery shares its space with the Rule's Pasco Poly tank manufacturing business. Judy, who is Gina Davis' aunt, takes care of the marketing, and Dave, who was raised in Middleton, makes the wine. An engineer by training, Dave's Pasco Poly began as a stainless steel tank business in Washington's Tri Cities. In 1986, the company began manufacturing plastic tanks and over the years crafted specialized equipment for the wine industry. Pasco Poly has sold tanks to winemakers all over North America and as far away as New Zealand.

While researching, he began making wine to "discover the ideal tank because it doesn't stratify...keeps the cap wet, keeps the temperature where you want and it's automatic." He learned as he went along. His new invention, the Pump-Under™ Fermentor, speeds the process. The wine still has to age, but the machine works quickly and cuts down on the labor. The couple use the fermentor in their own winemaking operation.

In 2008, the Rules started the winery to demonstrate their winemaking inventions. They began making reds for research. Today, they buy their grapes from Sunny Slope and Wilder, and they are in the business.

Their wines are made in the tanks and aged in the bottle. Their Rieslings have turned out very well. Remarkably, in their first year they've already won awards. The St. Regulus Reserve Riesling (under the name St. Rule) won a silver medal at the 2009 Idaho Wine Competition, and the winery won silver for Reserve Riesling and bronze for the Dry Riesling at 2009 Northwest Wine Summit. The Riesling also took a Best of Appellation Double Gold from *Appellation America*, which described the wine as a "fascinating and versatile food wine." St. Regulus plans to produce about 1,000 cases of Riesling, Rosé and Sparkling Rosé, as well as Cabernet Sauvignon, Merlot and Pinot Noir.

WINEMAKING INVENTIONS

Dave Rule, of St. Regulus Unique Wines, has been building wine tanks for 15 years. Pasco Poly SR Pump-Under™ Fermentor and pat. pending KiLR-CHiLR™ System are Rule's inventions. The Killer Chiller (KiLR-CHiLR™), an air-chilled poly tank, is an automated system for fermenting wines on the skins.

The Pump-Under™ Fermentor's made for reds, but "it does an excellent job on the whites," Dave says.

His tanks are virtually ubiquitous in Washington and Idaho and range in size from 100 to 4,300 gallons. They are air-cooled and are "extremely green" since they don't use any glycol.

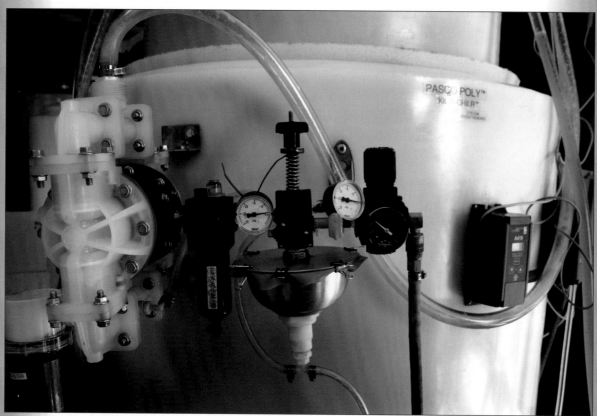

PASCO POLY. St. Regulus.

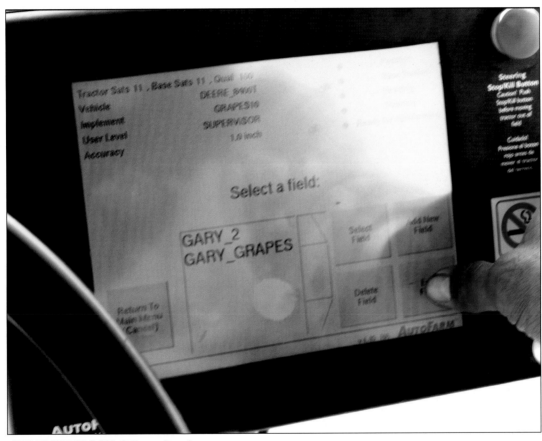

GPS TECHNOLOGY. 3 Horse Ranch.

3 HORSE RANCH. Bird netting, September.

3 HORSE RANCH. Brix testing.

BOTTLING. Carmela.

BOTTLING. Carmela.

CHAPTER NINE

TWIN FALLS, BUHL, GLENNS FERRY, HAGERMAN AND HAMMETT

F HEGY'S SOUTH HILLS WINERY

FRANK HEGY'S SOUTH HILLS WINERY BECAME LICENSED IN 1989. HIS TWIN FALLS VINEYARD, ABOUT AN ACRE, IS ONE OF THE FARTHEST EAST IN THE STATE. A NATIVE OF THE CALIFORNIA WINE COUNTRY, HEGY LEARNED ABOUT WINEMAKING FROM JAIME MARTIN (ROSE CREEK'S AND NOW COLD SPRINGS' WINEMAKER).

CHERUB. Carmela.

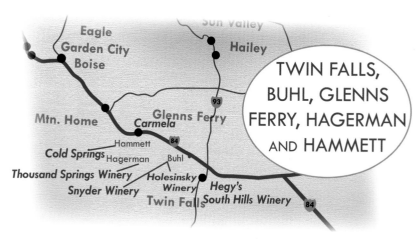

TWIN FALLS, BUHL, GLENNS FERRY, HAGERMAN AND HAMMETT

He's been in the restaurant business and now works in the heating business. His wine business has always been marked by his sense of humor. His Twin Falls residence and winemak-

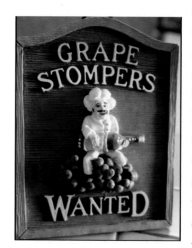

ing operation has some vintage equipment that includes a century-old press that still works and a 1946 Dodge pickup with his logo on it. Hegy buys most of his grapes locally and has been making wine for two decades. Operating on a small budget, Hegy says, "We use Mother Nature for the cold stabilization process. We couldn't afford the chilling equipment; we cold stabilize [outdoors] for three months," then the wines are filtered and bottled.

His trademark "Cheap Wine" was first done for personal use but developed a following. Back in the 1980s, he coined the name and got calls from all over. Cheap Wine was the first wine Hegy had approved; today they put this label on a Chardonnay, Merlot and Johannesburg Riesling, their largest production. "We pretty much stick to the sweeter wines because we do catering and a lot of special events," says Hegy.

The winery is a labor of love for Frank and Crystal Hegy. Hegy's has always done a fair amount of custom labeling, going

FRANK HEGY, WINEMAKER. Left: Sign at Hegy's South Hills Winery.

148

after "the specialty label market because it feeds into my catering business." The Hegys do weddings, golf tournaments, and some annual events and "can do barbecues for as many as 300 people." They're also in the landscape business, so it is hard to do tastings. No problem. They sell all the wine they make. Hegy says, "Every year when we are bottling we are out of wine.... We literally do everything, strictly a one-family operation." Bottling is the only thing that they get help with—it's a three-to-four person job. A tiny winery, Hegy's tends to stay in the 100-to-200 cases a year.

At Hegy's South Hills Winery, they do things the old-fashioned way. They grow grapes, tend their vines and continue to make Cheap Wine.

HOLESINSKY WINERY AND VINEYARD AND JAMES HOLESINSKY WINES

The Holesinsky Winery, just outside of Buhl, is evolving. James Holesinsky, who grows his grapes organically, makes some wines (about ten percent) that are organic, but under his new JH label most of his wines have some sulfites. He plans to always create wines from organic grapes and believes you should start with the fruit, the terroir and the soil. He states, "I don't use chemicals...I use the vineyard to make the wine." His vineyard and winery are both certified to produce and handle organic grapes and wine. Nothing is filtered.

Left: **JAMES HOLESINSKY.** Above: Merlot grapes, and **CHARDONNAY** with lady bugs.

In his early thirties, Holesinsky's one of Idaho's most unique vintners, the only grower in Idaho using biodynamic methods. Holesinsky went to school at the College of Southern Idaho, and then transferred to Davis to study enology and chemistry. He and his mom run a chemical products business for dairy farms in addition to the winery.

Holesinsky chose the spot for his vineyard on the family's historic farmland and, with his father's help, planted his 14 acres using furrow irrigation instead of drip lines.

Why furrows? Furrow irrigation drives roots deeper, "so you are accentuating the flavor from what's beneath the topsoil," he says. He likes to do his vineyard and winemaking the "hard way." Good pests— grasshoppers, praying mantises and ladybugs— keep the vineyard healthy and "drive out leaf hoppers and other bad pests." And he adds, "You have to have native grasses between the vines to create a home for the organic pests." Once they are established, "they are dominant."

Holesinsky raises syrah, merlot, chardonnay, muscat ottenel, and cabernet sauvignon as well as port varieties tinta cão, souzão, touriga; his altitude is about 2,900 feet, and he believes that syrah thrives in higher elevations. Holesinsky says, "I am to the extreme of ripening for bud break. You can't grow grapes any farther inland than here." Pruning is huge. "Every year is different," he adds. "When you have your own winery, you become neurotic and we are all perfectionists. You have to ripen your grapes at the right time and we can't ripen our grapes at the same time as California—period."

Balance is his mantra: "You have balance with soil, water, pruning your grapes, timing, weather and winemaking techniques, oak [he doesn't use new oak]. Everything has to be in balance with your technique in order for it to work." His winemaking is idiosyncratic too. Fermentation is extremely important; he propagates and grows his own yeasts. "I have a different method than a lot of people. I start in the vineyard and finish in the bottle...I use about six different yeasts for each different wine," he says. "The

complexity of the grapes tells me how I am going to make my wines."

He describes his method as in the French style, and adds he does "about ten times the cold soak" (about four weeks), so the wines pick up "volatile acidity" (VA) to create the flavor in the wines. A hint of VA gives the wine elegance, he asserts, adding, "The flavors are in the skins and in the fruit." He admires the French style. "The grapes have to be very, very ripe. I like depth and structure."

Holesinsky does about 800 to 900 cases a year—Riesling and Syrah, Merlot, a medley of Malbec, Syrah and Merlot, Rosé of Syrah from a vineyard in Hagerman. He sells out of his recently renovated tasting room (once the site of a milk tank), online, at the Boise Co-op and in wine stores. His wines are being noticed. Recent medals were awarded from the 2009 Idaho Wine Competition and the Northwest Wine Summit. The 2008 Rosé won double gold at the Idaho Wine Festival & Competition.

Ultimately, he contends that his central Idaho vineyard and those east of Canyon County should be in a separate AVA, because of the soil quality. As a member of a new generation of Gem State vintners, he is encouraged by the growth of the industry and firmly believes Idaho winemakers "have something to prove."

SNYDER WINE. Boise Co-op wines.

SNYDER WINERY, RESTAURANT AND TASTING ROOM

Originally called Blue Rock, Snyder Winery, Restaurant and Tasting Room are located a few miles from Buhl. Russ and Claudia Snyder own an 80-acre farm, where they raise cattle, have rainbow trout ponds and grow four varietals of grapes. They built their house and tasting room in 2004; it sits in a bucolic setting on the crest of a hill.

The Snyders' Tasting Room has a glorious rural view with the Soldier Mountains in the distance. During the spring and summer, the restaurant is open on weekends.

They bought the farm in 1999 and Claudia has been there most of the time ever since. Russ, who recently retired from the lumber business in Salt Lake City, has come back home. They did "a lot of site work" and the result is one of the more surprising destination wineries and tasting rooms. Claudia, who was in the interior design business in Salt Lake City, has created a comfortable setting to dine and sip wines.

The Snyders began growing grapes with a test vineyard in 2000, then began planting four acres in 2001; they grow riesling, syrah, cabernet franc and cabernet sauvignon. They also buy grapes from vineyards in Twin Falls and Hagerman. The Snyders self-distribute. Russ makes the wines, but the couple have used a consultant, Jim Yerkes out of Lodi, California, "who comes up once a year and does some blending for us," Russ says.

Grape growing has been an adventure for the Snyders, who quickly admit that they have been learning on the job.

CARMELA. Top: Winemaker Roger Jones.
Above: Tasting Room.

While they acknowledge their site at 3,700 feet is both a challenge (controlling the acids) and an advantage (intense sunlight), their farm sits in a relatively mild microclimate. The Snyders believe that they can make a very good wine on their sloping vineyard. They plan to make about 1,000 cases a year. Claudia, who has built the restaurant business and tasting room over the past years, sees the appellation (the AVA) as an important step in the state's reputation. They are conscious of their unique setting and have recently redesigned their labels. They've been hosting weddings for nine years and opened the restaurant five years ago.

They bottled their first wines in 2005 and are now selling their wines in Boise at the Co-op and the Atkinsons' markets throughout the Wood River Valley. Of course, they serve their wines with dinner at the restaurant. The steakhouse serves inch-thick steaks and also offers prime rib up to 32 ounces as well as rack of lamb and salmon. Snyder's restaurant is open on Fridays and Saturdays from 5:30 p.m. Reservations are required. They also have a cabin that they rent out for overnight stays.

CARMELA

Those who know Idaho potatoes from Idaho Baker's Dozen, the box of 13 beautiful russets that used to be sent nationwide, have Roger Jones to thank. The Jones' Idaho

CARMELA operations.

potatoes helped promote the state's most famous vegetable. The Jones family used to send 15 to 17 thousand boxes of "perfect potatoes," primarily during the holidays. Roger, who now owns Carmela, grew up in Rupert, where the Jones were renowned potato growers. A longtime member of the Idaho Potato Commission, Roger learned the business from his father, Rulon Jones, who was one of the larger suppliers of potato flakes.

The family farmed 8,000 acres and was also well-known for their fresh potatoes. For years, the Jones family owned a processing plant next door to Carmela in Glenns Ferry. Roger Jones sold out of the potato business in 2002, but continues to be involved in agriculture through his vineyard and winery.

Built in the mid-1980s, the Carmela winery has a capacity of 60,000 barrels. The vineyards date from the

1980s and have some of the oldest vines in southern Idaho. Roger Jones bought Carmela in June of 1997 from Jim and Candy Martell. The vineyards cover 30 acres and they raise chardonnay, riesling, semillon and merlot. Carmela's one of the few Idaho vineyards that grows lemberger. Jones also buys grapes from King Hill, Hagerman and from vineyards in southwestern Idaho.

The chateau-style winery sits amongst the vines, has a tasting room, gift shop, restaurant and golf course. Carmela makes 14 distinct wines and does about 14,000 cases per year, making it among the largest producers in the state. Wine varieties include Pinot Noir, Merlot, Chardonnay, Cabernet Sauvignon, Cabernet Franc, Cab-Merlot, Semillon, River Mist, Johannesburg Riesling, "Bodacious" Meritage (red) and a new Ice Wine. They sell about 75 percent of their wine on the premises and do a lot of private labeling—including an Obama wine and a Zen Red, made in honor of the Olympics in China. Their Njoy wines, which include a white, are named for Roger's late wife.

Carmela produces a number of less expensive wines. Jones believes the consumer is looking for better values. "We sell 80 percent of our wines from $8 to $15," he says. His business is growing, and he believes that the appellation is helping, especially "out of the state." Carmela sells mostly red wines, about four to one over the whites. He compares growing grapes to potatoes, and states: "It was pretty easy to sell Idaho potatoes, because it was one of the best-known vegetables in the world. When you tell someone we have a great wine from Idaho… we're not known for our wine but we are getting better at it."

Carmela is a destination winery and resort with a nine-hole golf course, restaurant, a full bar, and an RV Park, as well as cabins for rent. The restaurant features Idaho beef and fish from the West Coast, and hosts a series of winemaker-themed dinners including Mardi Gras, a Cowboy Formal, an Asian night and crab feeds—all with wine paired with different dishes. The drive from Boise takes about an hour; in the warm months food is served indoors and outdoors.

The winery sits next to Three Island State Park and is popular for weddings and celebrations. It's a grand spot for a picnic or a day trip. Carmela's elevation is 2,525 and the vineyards overlook the Snake River. The view from the winery and restaurant is one of the most exquisite in southern Idaho.

THOUSAND SPRINGS WINERY AND VINEYARD

Nestled on the banks of the Snake River, Thousand Springs Winery has a small vineyard with a grand view of the Snake River. Winemaker Paul Monahan, an emergency room physician who travels around the region, calls his operation a "boutique winery." Monahan, who used to live in Sun Valley, still works as an emergency room doctor full time; he's been an interstate commuter since 1977.

He raises grapes as a hobby and went into the winemaking business because he couldn't sell his crop in 2001. He bought his ten acres, which are covered in vineyards and orchards, and started growing grapes. Monahan actually

began with table grapes, still has some concord and Thompson seedless that he and his wife keep for themselves and the local birds. Monahan crafts about 400 cases per annum. Other than his Rosé, all his wines are aged in oak and done with one-hundred-percent varietals.

The winery and handsomely renovated tasting room reside in the former barn. All the doors are antique and there's a glorious 13-foot spruce serving table. Monahan has a collection of antique harvesting tools that he still puts to use.

Thousand Springs Winery uses a machine called "a Killer Chiller" (from Pasco Poly) to cold stabilize his wines. The Chardonnay undergoes cold fermentation and aging at 55 degrees for up to a year. The wines age in Hungarian oak. Currently, Monahan offers a Chardonnay and a Cabernet-Franc/Syrah that's a 50/50 blend as well as a Rosé of Syrah. The first offering of his oak-aged Syrah will be a 2005 vintage. Licensed and bonded in 2005, Thousand Springs Winery sells locally at the Snake River Grill in Hagerman, in New Vintage in Meridian, at the Wine

TASTING ROOM. Thousand Springs Winery.

Garden in Blackfoot, as well as in The Seasons in Eagle, the Boise Co-op and at Brick 29 in Nampa.

Monahan calls Cinder's Melanie Krause his "mentor." She has consulted on the winemaking for about two years and recommended the barrels he uses. He prides himself on crafting "un-tweaked wines." A candid man, he believes that Idaho wines should be distinct. "An Idaho Chardonnay is not a California Chardonnay," he says. "It's neither over-oaked nor [tastes of] stainless steel." Monahan enjoys all parts of the process of growing grapes and making the wine, but doesn't relish marketing.

The Thousand Springs Winery, about ten miles east of Hagerman, is owned by Monahan and his wife, Susan Parslow. Monahan grows his own grapes on his two-acre vineyard but also buys local grapes. His 2006 Chardonnay won a gold medal in the 2008 Idaho Wine Competition, and Monahan adds, "They may come to kick the tires but no one leaves here without buying my Rosé."

COLD SPRINGS WINERY

The Cold Springs Winery and Vineyard has a distinctive sign that stretches across the roof of a storage building north of I-84, just before the Hammett exit. It shouldn't be a total surprise that Bill Ringert's winery sign can almost be seen by passing aircraft given his background as a pilot in the U.S. Air Force. Ringert and his effervescent wife Bing have been married for five decades and own and operate the Cold Springs Winery, a little less than an hour's drive from Boise.

A graduate of the University of Idaho and Castleford native, Bill went to law school at Southern Methodist University and has had a long and distinguished career as a lawyer—specializing in the last 20 years of his career in wa-

ter law. He served six years in the Idaho State Senate (1983-1988). The Ringerts lived in Boise, but Bill always had an eye for land in the country. They found the farm originally in 1985 and moved to Hammett in 1996. The winery takes its name from nearby Cold Springs Creek. Bill and Bing planted

BILL RINGERT. Cold Springs Tasting Room.

the first acre of grapes together. Most of their acreage was planted between 1998 and 2004. The farm totals 260 acres.

In 2002, the Ringerts decided to build a winery; soon they hired Jaime Martin who raises grapes in Hagerman. They became licensed in 2003. Currently, they produce just fewer than 4,000 cases per year. Bill expects "to eventually get up to about 8,500 cases." Most of Cold Springs' wines are single varietals; they do a second brand they call Hot Rod Red that's a blend of cab franc, syrah and merlot that come from Martin's vineyard.

With the able help of pioneer winemaker Martin, who owned Rose Creek Winery, and vineyard manager Julia Heath, Cold Springs has been making wines for the past five years. The Ringerts' daughter Beth has recently joined the business to direct marketing. The high altitude vineyards (2,700 feet and higher) cover 33 acres, and Ringert raises nine grape varietals: riesling, chardonnay, pinot gris, viognier, cabernet sauvignon, merlot, pinot noir, syrah, and tempranillo.

"Everything about raising grapes is fascinating to me," Ringert says. He thought that going into the wine business would allow him and Bing to travel to California and France and visit with others in the business. His greatest surprise has been how much time the work takes. He quickly adds that driving the tractor under the wide Idaho sky "is kind of inspirational for someone of an agricultural bent," and adds, "It's different than watching a combine cut down wheat." Ringert allows that winemaking is an ongoing process with lots of checking and testing. Picking is done by hand in his vineyard, and he particularly enjoys the process from harvest to crush.

Easily accessible off I-84, the tasting room has a unique high desert view; it's a pleasant place to sample wine and peer out over the vineyards.

The tasting room is Bing Ringert's domain. A natural saleswoman and conversationalist, asked the difference between politics and winemaking, Bing replies, "In winemaking, it's a lot easier to please the people than it is in politics." She believes the Idaho wine industry is on its way, winks and says, "Grapes are like Idahoans; they like to struggle."

BILL RINGERT. Cold Springs Winery.

WINTER. Hells Canyon Winery.

HELLS CANYON WINERY.

COLD SPRINGS WINERY.

Frenchman's Gulch. Winter.

CHAPTER TEN

KETCHUM

FRENCHMAN'S GULCH WINERY

Ketchum, Idaho may be best known as the town next to the Sun Valley Resort and the home to Bald Mountain, Idaho's premier ski hill. But tucked at the end of 9th Street beneath the shadow of Knob Hill, Frenchman's Gulch Winery and Tasting Room, elevation 5,750 feet, occupies a site that defines high-altitude winemaking.

On a bright winter day, few places can compare to the intimate tasting room in this picturesque stone and wood building with its oak barrel hoist affixed to the front gable. In this unlikely setting to make premium vintages, Frenchman's Gulch has blended an award-winning 2005 Cuvée, crafted 2005 Merlot, Syrah, Cabernet Sauvignon, and its 2006 Chardonnay. From the courtyard, a wine taster can watch skiers corkscrew their runs down Baldy.

WINEMAKER STEVE "MAC" MCCARTHY.

FRENCHMAN'S GULCH.
Open.

Next door are the barrel room, winery and warehouse where the patient art of winemaking occurs. Frenchman's Gulch ages wines in French, Hungarian and American oak barrels.

A Chicago transplant, winemaker Steve "Mac" McCarthy first experimented making wine 25 years ago when he tended a half-acre vineyard in Michigan not far from the lake. He and his wife Tracey moved to Ketchum 16 years ago. Mac and Tracey began their boutique winery in 1998 in their garage; the first release was in 2000. He quips, "I started in my garage with two tons of grapes and 14 barrels, stayed there until my wife kicked me out." Tracey designed the two-story building, employing earth colors reminiscent of Knob Hill on the exterior, and created

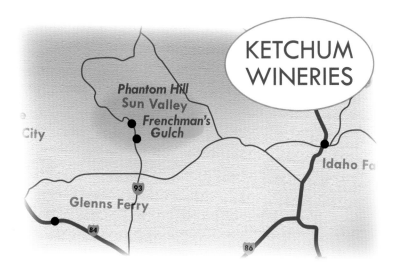

KETCHUM WINERIES

Mac sees advantages to high-country winemaking. He believes "the wines are softer and easier drinking [smoother] because of the altitude." They often press in the snow, and less oxygen contributes to flavor too. He smiles when he says, "there's no protein" in his wines (fruit flies can't live at 6,000 feet). Frenchman's Gulch has evolved. In 2003, the winery produced just 180 cases. The 2005 releases added up to about 1,200 cases.

This mile-high operation received a lot of attention in 2008. Frenchman's Gulch took home three medals from the Northwest Wine Summit held in Mt. Hood, Oregon. The 2005 Ketchum Cuvée took first place for "best Bordeaux blend under $30," the 2005 Syrah won a silver medal, and the 2005 Merlot won a bronze.

The name is not the only reminder of Old World winemaking. Frenchman's Gulch makes red wines in the Bordeaux-style; the 2005 Cuvée blends cabernet sauvignon (52 percent), merlot (28 percent) and cabernet franc (20 percent). *Wine Press Northwest's* website made it their wine of the week on May 6, 2008. The Merlot, Syrah and Chardonnay are true expressions of handcrafted wines made in thin air.

an inviting and cozy tasting room. Mac built it and created the 1,300-square foot winemaking operation across the courtyard.

The grapes come from Washington vineyards, including Dwelley and Horse Heaven Hills. Mac visits the vineyards often, buys by the acre, prefers modest yields of two-and-a-half to three-and-a-half tons and has developed a business-by-handshake relationship with the growers. Everything is done by hand. After he picks up the grapes from Walla Walla and Yakima, he drives them to Ketchum on a flatbed truck. Once the grapes arrive, the process becomes a community affair. Friends and family help crush, hand-punch and basket-press the varietals. Finally, the juice goes through fermentation, and is barrel-aged, usually for two years. (It takes wines longer in higher altitude.) The labels are applied, the bottles corked and sealed with wax.

PHANTOM HILL

When locals refer to Phantom Hill, they usually mean the steep rise just north of Ketchum. It's also the name of a local wolf pack that wanders central Idaho, but to wine aficionados the name represents one of Idaho's best wines but least-known brands. Owner and winemaker Anthony Maratea describes Phantom Hill as "the winery without a winery," says that as a winemaker he's "like a guy without a country."

Maratea moved to Ketchum from Massachusetts in 1976 and soon went to work wholesaling wine. In 1978, he founded Nouveaux Distributing in Ketchum, which he sold in 2007 to Stein Distribution. He still retains an office there but no longer manages the day-to-day operation. Maratea's one of the few people in Northwest winemaking who has been on all sides of the industry as a winemaker, a grape grower and a wholesaler.

Phantom Hill's story begins in 1996. Encouraged by the late Gary Andrus (the legendary winemaker who owned Pine Ridge Winery in California and Archery Summit in Oregon), Maratea brought a small amount of Kirby Vickers' chardonnay grapes and began his career making wine. His plan had been to make 50 cases of Chardonnay. But with more encouragement from Andrus, he also made 1,150 cases of Pinot Noir with Oregon fruit. Archery Summit helped with distribution and, almost immediately, Phantom Hill's wines were selling in 15 or 16 states.

Since he launched his label in 1996, Phantom Hill has offered from time to time a much-admired Chardonnay as

Photo by Roxanne Minskoff

WINEMAKER ANTHONY MARATEA holds a bottle of Phantom Hill 2003 Pinot Noir.

well as a fine Pinot Noir and recently a Pinot Gris; Maratea has sourced grapes from Idaho— from the Wood River Canyon Vineyard, Dr. John Ocker's Kuna Butte Vineyard and from Sawtooth—as well as from Oregon. His wines are offered in restaurants like Beverly's at the Coeur d'Alene Resort, and various spots in the Wood River Valley. He thought of the name on a drive to Oregon when he "saw a rising phoenix on the back of a truck." Maratea had listed three pages of possible names, but he settled on Phantom Hill because of his ties to the Wood River Valley.

Like Andrus' wines, Phantom Hill uses all new oak barrels whether red or white; Maratea likes "oaky wines" but doesn't want the oak to be "overwhelming." From the shape of his bottles to his winemaking technique, he emulates the Burgundian style.

"As far as the future goes, I have 450 cases worth of Dundee Hills Pinot Noir and Idaho Pinot Noir," he says. And he still has some of his Revelation Pinot Noir that comes from a vineyard that he co-owned with Andrus. Like the phoenix that he saw when he came up with the name, Anthony Maratea's making wine again. Available locally in the Wood River Valley and at select outlets, it may not be easy to locate but it's worth seeking.

FRENCHMAN'S GULCH. Tasting room.

CHARDONNAY at harvest.

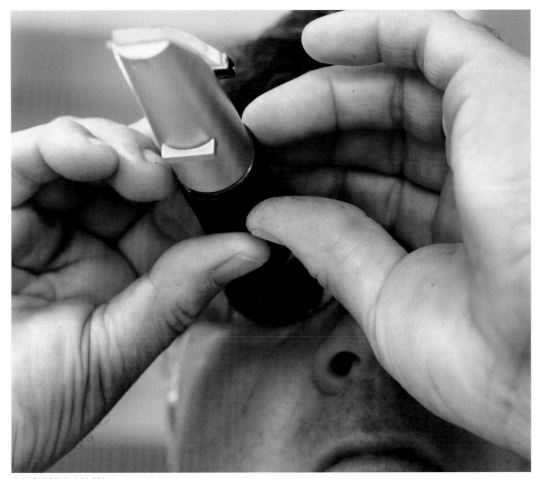

3 HORSE RANCH. Brix.

VERAISON. Changing colors.

THOUSAND SPRINGS WINERY AND VINEYARD.

CONCLUSION

ECONOMIC IMPACT

While modest compared to Oregon and Washington, the economic impact of Idaho grapes and wineries shows a distinctly upward trend. Despite the recent downturn in the economy, Idaho wine sales went up, the number of wineries grew and the acreage in wine grapes expanded.

In December of 2008, the Idaho Grape Growers and Wine Producers Commission released a study ("The Economic Impact of the Wine Industry on Idaho's Economy" by Kristin Bierle, Donald Holley, Geoffrey Black of Boise State University, Center for Business and Economic Research) that showed an industry coming into its own:

- The Idaho wine industry represents an annual $73 million total economic impact.

MOYA SHATZ, Idaho Wine Producers Commission, Executive Director.

- $52 million in annual winery revenues.
- The industry employs 625 people directly and indirectly.
- Generates $3.1 million in state tax revenues.
- Sales increased by 3.3 percent in 2008.

The study goes on to point out that wineries grew from just 11 in 2002 to 38 in 2008 (today the number is about 40) and that the growth of wineries "has led to increased visibility of Idaho wines and increased tourism." Centered in Canyon County, Idaho wine country promotes the region's historic commitment to agriculture, provides jobs and gives the region an identity for wine travelers.

The United States has about 6,000 wineries, ranks number four in the world in wine production; consumption has grown from about a gallon per capita in 1970 to more than three in 2007. The United States is second in the world for wine consumption.

In 2001, Idaho produced 166,000 cases; that amount rose to 230,000 in 2007 and is probably about 250,000 today. Wine grapes are second in acreage and third in value for Idaho fruit. The study predicts that Idaho wineries should double by 2015, and acreage devoted to wine grapes will expand by about 1,000 acres. Revenues will be closer to $80 million. Commenting on the industry's growth, Moya Shatz, executive director of the Idaho Wine Commission wrote:

> Wine business [in 2009] has been good. We saw eight new wineries open; lots of visitors in the summer had an amazing wine event, Savor Idaho, in June. We defeated the beer and wine tax and are working diligently to improve our rules and regulations. The best thing is more and more local Idahoans are drinking Idaho wine.

Judging by the extraordinary response to the inaugural Savor Idaho, where about 600 people sampled dozens of Idaho wines, and the growth of the industry throughout the state, the best days for Idaho winemakers and grape growers are just ahead.

On the Horizon

New wineries are in the works. Greg Alger's Huston Vineyards, in the historic corner of Sunny Slope, already has fruit-bearing vines in a lovely spot. Expect the Clearwater region to add more vineyards and new wineries. In the Palouse, editor and writer Tim Steury's growing all manner of cider apples and before long he intends to produce a French-style hard cider. Sheppard Fruit Wines in Harrison and the activity in Eagle bode well.

Stay tuned, consult Facebook, go on Twitter, and listen. Those popping sounds you hear from Idaho mean new vintages are being opened, purple and gold liquids swirled and Northwest wines enjoyed.

PUG OSTLING, owner of Grape Escape, Boise, with a bottle of Fraser's 2007 Cabernet Sauvignon.

ACKNOWLEDGEMENTS

T HIS BOOK WOULD NOT HAVE BEEN POSSIBLE WITHOUT THE FULL COOPERATION OF IDAHO'S WINEMAKERS AND GRAPE GROWERS. FIRST, WE WANT TO EXPRESS OUR GRATITUDE TO THE IDAHO GRAPE GROWERS AND WINE PRODUCERS COMMISSION. AT EVERY TURN, EXECUTIVE DIRECTOR MOYA SHATZ PROVIDED INSIGHT, HELP AND DID FIRST-RATE POURS.

During the year and a half it took to create this book, we came to know dozens of winemakers, grape growers, people inside and outside the industry who invariably were hospitable and helpful. Everyone we talked to in the Idaho wine community freely shared their time and insights.

Since the book was on Idaho wines, we focused on winemakers and their efforts. We are grateful to the following winemakers and grape growers and others who we interviewed for the book: Ron Bitner, Mike Crowley, Gary and Martha Cunningham, John Danielson, Gina and George Davis, Tim Day, Chuck Devlin, Dick Dickstein, Scott DeSeelhorst, Bill Fraser, Martin Fujishin, Kimber Gates and Warren Schutz, Neil Glancey, Frank Hegy, James

Holesinsky, Greg and Andrew Koenig, Melanie Krause and Joe Schnerr, Roger L. Jones, Ted Judd, Lloyd Mahaffey, Anthony Maratea, Ken McCabe, Mike McClure, Steve Meyer, Steve "Mac" McCarthy, Tracey McCarthy, Jim and Michele Mitchell, Paul Monahan, Bill Murray, Mike Pearson and Melissa Sanborn, Leslie Preston, Angie Riff, Bill and Bing Ringert, Steve and Leslie, Bijou and Hadley Robertson, Michelle Rogers, Dave Rule, Stu and Sue Scott, Moya Shatz, Jim Sheppard, Claudia and Russ Snyder, Sabrina Snodderley, Bill Stowe, Tammy Stowe, Tim Steury, Patty and Tim Switzer, Jo Ann Hansen, Gary Rencehausen, Dick Symms and Dar Symms, Coco and Carl Umiker, Kirby and Cheryl Vickers, Cheyne Weston and Roger Williamson.

We want to thank the folks at the Orchard House for letting us use their restaurant as a field office, the members of the Canyon County Economic Development Council for letting us sit in on their meetings. We first mentioned our idea to Caxton's Scott Gipson at Caldwell's Music of the Vine, one of wine country's best places to taste local vintages. Thanks to Beth and Gary Beard and their partners at Music of the Vine for letting us use their premises to conduct interviews and have meetings. Thanks to Nancy Gordon for help finding websites and information.

We also need to express our gratitude to: Pug Ostling, who has long serenaded Idaho wines from the Grape Escape in Boise; to the wine gang at the Boise Co-op, especially David Kirkpatrick, who was our wine writer at Boise Magazine, Divit Cardoza, whose dedication to Idaho wines has helped reshape the tastes and attitudes of a generation of local wine drinkers and Todd Geisler, who has left the wine gang but remains at the Co-op, who orchestrated a trip to the California wine country more than a decade ago. Krista Shellie of the University of Idaho Extension at Parma generously showed us her operation and aided with technical information and real-world research on Idaho viticulture. Jack Peterson shared his insights into soil and geology. Ron Bitner deserves special mention for helping to nurture this book and the Idaho wine industry. We would be remiss not to mention the marvelous meal (and revealing blind tastings) we had at Hells Canyon. And thanks to the Vickers for the lovely spread they put out for us. Thanks to Marilyn Sabella for her insights into Sandpoint; and to Ivar, Pat and Katrina Nelson for a memorable dinner in Moscow.

Portions of the text appeared in a different form online in NewWest.net, and in the following magazines: *Boise Journal*, *Horizon Air Magazine*, *McCall*, *3C* and *Boise Home and Garden*. We want to thank editors Jill Kuraitis, Christine Evangelides and Michelle Andrus for their insights and suggestions. Doug Copsey shared resources and thoughts about the project.

We both tip our glasses to Skip Oppenheimer for taking the time to fly Paul around the valley to get aerial photographs of the vineyards and countryside. Ste. Chapelle's Chuck Devlin deserves our thanks for giving multiple interviews and showing Paul some of his favorite wine country spots. Thanks from Paul also go to: Royal Borough of Kensington and Chelsea Councillor Barry Phelps and James Dufficy in London, photographer Hugh Routledge, also in London, Mom and sister Jane in London, and New York Times photographer Stephen Crowley in Washington D.C.; so many wonderful editors in New York and the inimitable Harry Hamburg; Randy Pearce at Timeless Photo in Boise and Gary Daniel at the Idaho Capitol Commission. Many, too numerous to name, were generous and intuitively understood that to photograph this wonderful state and its spirited people required more than just a half-hearted welcome.

Our editor, Judy Steele, provided gentle but firm guidance. She carefully edited the text, smoothed the prose and managed the project. And we greatly appreciate the talented Chris Latter, whose design work on this and previous Caxton books is extraordinary. She proved to be an invaluable member of the team. Thanks to Wayne Cornell for his excellent work on our index. A special thanks to Melanie Krause, who graciously fact checked the glossary. We also want to thank Scott Gipson for his unflagging support of our work and all his help on this book.

Finally, we are most grateful to our wives, Royanne Minskoff and Gaye Bennett, who both signed on early, joined us at events and logged many solitary hours, while their husbands traversed the state. We are thankful for all the help but any errors belong to us.

GLOSSARY

Ag-tourism ~ A way to see where food is grown and purchase local products.

Alcohol and Tobacco Tax and Trade Bureau (TTB) ~ replaced the BATF as the governmental entity responsible for administration of the wine and spirits industries.

Appellation ~ A designated wine grape-growing region governed by a set of standards.

Appellation of origin in the United States ~ means that the wine comes from as many as three contiguous states, or counties. In order for a wine to use the term on a label it must meet specific requirements for the percentage of grapes and where they are grown.

AVA American Viticultural Area ~ This system is similar to France's appellation designation. Defined as a specific geographical area, an AVA designated wine has to have 85 percent of its grapes from that region.

Biodynamic methods ~ A viticulture system that works in sync with the movement of the planets. Soils are infused with plant, mineral or animal material according to the alignment of the planets.

Bladder press ~ Generally considered an improvement over the wooden-basket ratchet-style press and is a gentler method for juice extraction. After a rubber bladder expands, fruit is pushed to the sides of the cage.

Blocks ~ Designated varietal areas in the vineyard.

Brix ~ Scale of measurement that U.S. wine growers use to determine the sugar content in grapes and wine.

Brut ~ Driest sparkling wines with less residual sugar than those described as "extra dry."

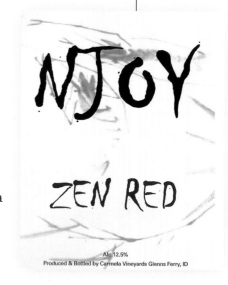

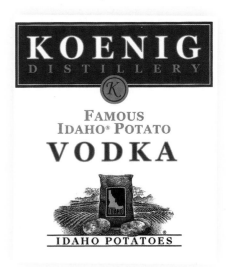

Bud break ~ Normally occurs in April and signals the start of the grape-growing season. It is usually about 100 days from bud break until veraison.

Canopy management ~ Includes vine spacing, pruning, thinning, leaf removal and shoot positioning as well as trellising and virtually any detail of managing the air and light that affects the grapes.

Canopy balance ~ Balancing the fruit clusters and leaves for optimal sugars and flavor.

Cap ~ Skins and seeds that float above the liquid in a fermentor.

Cluster thinning ~ Removing excess clusters or bunches.

Cold soaked ~ Sometimes called cold maceration, a process where the grape juice is cooled quickly, then held for a time—a week or more—before fermentation.

2004
Reserve Merlot
King Hill Vineyard, Idaho

Crop heavy ~ The grape grower takes a higher tonnage per acre from the vineyard.

Cultivar ~ Synonym for grape varietal.

Cuvée ~ Term designating a blended wine. The word cuve in French means vat.

Davis ~ The University of California at Davis', famed enology program has produced many of the country's most eminent winemakers and is a center for viticulture studies and research.

Deficit irrigation ~ Watering method that grape growers use to control growth of the canopy and the size of the berry.

Degree-days ~ The University of California at Davis system of quantifying the heat units that vines receive.

FRASER
VINEYARD

2005
IDAHO

CABERNET
SAUVIGNON

ALC. 14.5% BY VOL.

Weston

2001
IDAHO
Merlot

Alcohol 12% by Volume

Disgorged or disgorgement ~ Stage in méthode Champenoise where sediment is removed from the wine.

Drip irrigation ~ Method of watering plants using plastic pipes that release monitored small amounts of water to the plant.

Eau de vie ~ Clear fruit-based brandy.

Enology ~ Study of wines and winemaking.

Esters ~ Chemical compounds that are produced during fermentation induced by the reaction of alcohol to acids—thought to make wines mores complex.

Free run ~ Juice that comes from grapes that have not been pressed.

Fruit-forward wine ~ Sometimes called fruit-driven, generally means that the wine's predominant flavors are lush and opulent with hints of fruit as opposed to earthy or floral.

Hand-riddled ~ Traditional method for removing dead yeast cells from sparkling wine that shifts the bottles

to an upside down position at a 45-degree angle every few days.

Kueka ~ Refers to Kueka Lake, a wine grape region in New York state's Finger Lakes. Kueka Lake is located near the town of Hammondsport and vineyards were established there in the 19th century.

Leaf cutting bees ~ Named for the distinctive patterns they cut out of leaves used for their nests; they are excellent pollinators whose introduction into Australia dramatically increased alfalfa seed yields.

Malolactic ~ Secondary fermentation that converts malic acid into lactic acid and carbon dioxide. This process is commonly done in red wines to soften them, but is not used in whites.

Méthode Champenoise ~ The traditional method of making sparkling wine in France's Champagne region. This style, in English called the "champagne method," includes taking still wines and making a blend, "cuvée,"

of many wines to determine the champagne vintner's house style. This complex cuvée can have as many as 40 different wines.

Must ~ The grape juice that will be fermented into wine and can contain pulp, stems, skin and seeds.

Off dry ~ Wines with only the slightest hint of sweetness.

Old Vines ~ Not a formal designation but means that the grapes are grown on vines for 25 years old or more. It implies smaller yields and finer fruit.

Phylloxera (root louse) ~ A tiny insect that attacks the roots of grape vines, especially vitis vinifera (which accounts for most of the world's wine grapes). Also known as vine aphids, these pests are considered to be the cause of European grape vine devastation in the 19th century. California grape growers have also had infestations. It is thought that Idaho vineyards have not suffered because cold winters here mitigate against these insects.

Post-destemmer sorting machine ~ Adds an additional sorting step to select the best grapes.

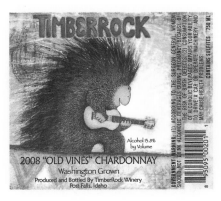

Punch ~ Often called "punching down," refers to pushing the cap down into the juice during fermentation.

Refractometer ~ Measures the amount of sugars in grapes or in the must. This measurement is recorded in brix.

Source or sourcing grapes ~ The place a vintner or winemaker gets his or her wine grapes.

Tannins ~ Harsh elements in red wines that derive from the stems, seeds, and skins and can occur in wines aged in oak. Tannic wines can have an astringent taste and many winemakers work to soften or achieve ripe tannins. Tannins do soften with aging.

Terroir ~ French word for soil that signifies the specific qualities of a wine-growing region and all the factors—altitude, climate, environment, and soil composition—that affect the quality of the wines.

Two-shoot training ~ Vine trellis method used, giving a second shoot to the grape grower if something goes awry with the first.

Varietal ~ Predominant grape in a wine.

Veraison ~ Transition time when berries ripen, soften and begin to turn from green to either red or yellow.

Vertical shoot positioning (VSP) trellis system ~ Growing shoots are trained between pairs of catch wires on either side of the post to the top of the trellis. When shoots reach the top of the trellis they then can be trimmed off to stop shading. VSP promotes proper leaf canopy and allows for good fruit development.

Vintage ~ Year the grapes were picked and the wine was made. In the United States the vintage signifies that 95 percent of the grapes were picked in the year on the label.

Vintner ~ Person who makes and/or sells wines.

Viticulture ~ Wine grape cultivation, implies the study of the techniques and methods of raising grapes.

Vitis Vinifera ~ Vine species from which 99 percent of all the wine grapes grown on the planet originate; all the wine world's most important grape varietals trace their lineage to this species.

INDEX

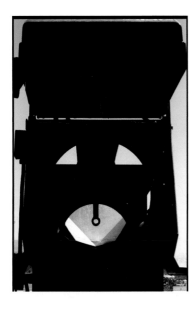

D

E

F

G

H

I

J

JAGUAR loves Hells Canyon Winery.

GLASSES. Davis Creek Cellars.

Alan Minskoff - biography

Alan Minskoff teaches journalism and writing at the College of Idaho, where he has directed the Journalism minor since 2004. The longtime editor of *Boise Magazine*, he was the editorial director of *Boise Journal* and *ArtIdaho* magazines from 2001 until 2004. He was the editor of *The Constitution at 200: Idaho Perspectives* and editor-in-chief for *Here We Have Idaho: People Make the Difference*. He wrote *Keeping the Faith*, a history of Boise's Ahavath Beth Israel congregation, and has written dozens of articles about Idaho since moving to the state in 1972. He teaches in the Cabin's Summer Writing Camp and has taught in the Writers in the Schools program. His poetry has appeared in *Eight Idaho Poets* (University of Idaho Press, 1978); *Idaho's Poetry: A Centennial Anthology* (University of Idaho Press, 1988); *Things to do in Idaho* (Blue Scarab Press, 1990); and in two chapbooks - *Blue Ink Runs Out on a Partly Cloudy Day* (1994) and *Point Blank* (2006), both from Limber-lost Press. He has written about Idaho wine for *Horizon Air*, *Boise Journal*, and *McCall* and recently blogged about it on NewWest.net. He is married to Royanne Minskoff, has three children - Noah, Hank and Laura - and lives in Boise.

WAX PATTERN. Davis Creek Cellars.

Paul Hosefros - biography

Paul Hosefros, who retired as senior photographer in Washington D.C. for the *New York Times*, blames Bordeaux. In his early 20s and not long graduated from New York University, he was already working for the *Times* in New York when he was invited to work on wine stories with a columnist in France. Three weeks of intense research - including visits to Haut Brion and lunch at Mouton with Baron Philippe himself - gave Paul not just a world-class beginning education...but also a headache. In the intervening years, he's worked with the late Craig Claiborne, and photographed war zones, fires, models, seven Presidents, countless foreign heads of state, earthquakes, hurricanes and sports. He has been published not just in the *Times* but in numerous other publications. Now "retired" in Idaho and a proud Master degree graduate from Boise State University, Paul has come full circle with this wine book.

He says: When we consider Idaho, we often simply see the grand mountains and "big sky" vistas of the state. Yet, to me, we experience the fields and rivers in an up-close, personal way - the crunch of volcanic soil beneath our feet, the wind gripping our coattails, the personal taste of fruits, of vegetables...of wine. So, as you consider these photos, consider that each tries by close-ups with a macro lens and broad, wide-angled vistas to help you experience both the vast power of Idaho and its delicious details.

Paul is married to Gaye Bennett and they have a son, Brian, a music composer. They reside in Caldwell.

DRINKING LOCALLY
- Alan Minskoff

Idaho Viogniers taste like cool jazz on hot summer nights. Purple and velvety Sunny Slope Syrahs thrive in high desert. Attitude and altitude mark our wines. Vines hover above the Snake River as it winds its way west to the Pacific and eternity. Blue-black and gold clusters have returned to the Clearwater. On a July eve, gaze at the glorious Panhandle lake country. Clink glasses, swirl the yellow liquid from grapes grown in the southwest's cinder and cobble-strewn soil, but crafted in downtown Sandpoint, then sniff, sip and savor a crisp Pend d'Oreille Chardonnay.

SUNDAY CONCERTS at Ste. Chapelle

WINERY

WINEMAKER

DATE

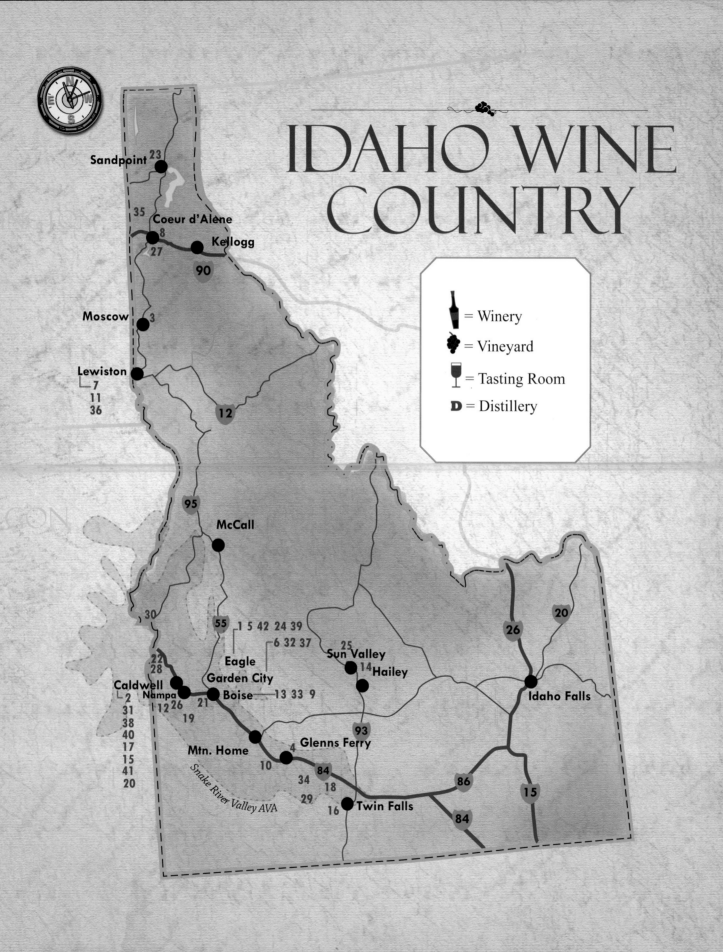

IDAHO WINE COUNTRY

Sandpoint 23

35

Coeur d'Alene
8
27 Kellogg
90

Moscow 3

Lewiston
7
11
36

12

95

McCall

= Winery

= Vineyard

= Tasting Room

D = Distillery

30

55   1 5 42 24 39

6 32 37

25
Sun Valley
14 Hailey

22
28

Eagle
Garden City

Caldwell
2
31
38
40
17
15
41
20

Nampa
12 26
19

Boise   13 33 9

21

20

26

Idaho Falls

93

Glenns Ferry

Mtn. Home
10

4

84

34
29

18

86

15

Snake River Valley AVA

16 Twin Falls

84